“The Fighting Rose”

By

Faith Divine

ISBN: 978-0-578-85971-2

First printing 2021

Acknowledgments

I want to thank God again, for helping me to prepare part two of My Life and My Struggles. In writing this part of this book, He has worked much patience in me as well as shown me just how tough life can be.

I want to thank my children for their patience and helping me to be able to adjust writing this part. Through my daughter, Monique, God has allowed me to see her strengths; and as a mother, has taught me much guidance. She has shown great strength and the ability to endure hardships as a good soldier. Her mind and her ways of thinking has reshaped me as a mother, although she is a mother herself.

My oldest son, Corey, has shown much love and patience through all of enduring his trials and tribulations. His strength and his faith in God has shown me another level of God's protection and patience.

My second son, Kevin, and middle child, he has the faith that I have never seen. He tells me that he got what he called, “”crazy faith” from me. But little did he realize, his faith has helped me to rebuild mine.

I can truly say that I thank God for my children and how I have seen them grow up to become parents themselves and the strength they have endured in raising their own children.

I want to tell them, “thank you.”

Everyone else who will take the time to read this book, I want you to think about your situation and ways you can help build who you are.

Thank you!

Contents

Chapter One

"My Move"

I had escaped the abuse from my former spouse, some family members and from the church. I also escaped the grief of my sister's death. As I entered a new phase of my life, there were many adjustments I had to make. One of those being the need to reconnect with my family.

Over the Christmas holiday, I decided to go to Georgia to comfort my granddaughter who was having a difficult time dealing with the loss of her mother, whose birthday was on Christmas.

As I returned to Florida, a friend of mine picked me up from the airport. When she picked me up, she informed me that someone had been murdered on the street behind where I lived.

I later discovered that the homicide did actually occur right behind where I lived. This news was devastating to me because I was an easy target. I lived alone, I was on crutches as a result of knee surgery, and although I had a dog, it was a small Maltese. He would indicate whether it was safe to go outside, but he could not offer physical protection. Due to my vulnerability, my sister suggested I would be safer living with her.

I didn't immediately move with her and upon returning back to Florida, I was scheduled to return to work the next day. Since it was my first evening to return to work since my surgery, I felt that I should not try to work the entire eight hours, but work only four, so I could work my way back into the full eight-hour shift comfortably. When I returned home that evening, pulling up into my driveway and upon entering into my house, I immediately heard gunshots.

I knew that it had to be God for me to have only worked four hours that evening. I realized then, that I had a choice to either stay there or make a change. And I chose to get away from the area (*this rose was fighting for safety).*

This is when I moved in with my sister in Georgia. I was just getting off of my crutches and was still having a hard time dealing with pain from my surgery. My sister had a steep driveway and I would try to walk down and up again for the exercise to help strengthen my knee. It was very difficult at first, but then it was beginning to help (this rose was fighting for recovery).

During this time, I wasn't employed, so I would work around the house, sell dinners and do chores in the home to help her out so my stay there wasn't a free one.

Although she said that it was ok, knowing that I didn't have income coming in, I did not want to be a burden.

Well, my dinners sold, and then I started doing other things. I finally obtained employment after being there for about two months. I started working for an agency that helped with juvenile males and females adjusting to life's problems.

These were personal homes owned by the agency and about 6 youths were in each of the four homes. I enjoyed working with the youth. My first house I was assigned to was about 40 minutes from where I lived. And for some reason, my female employer was not a nice person to get along with. It was as if she was struggling with her own insecurities or even struggles with something that had happened in her past. It almost seemed as if she wanted some type of revenge to inflict on someone. I really felt sorry for her in a way because I knew deep within, she was a kind and compassionate person.

I remember when she asked me to work the summer program; I did everything she asked me. I watched how she did it and did things as I saw her do them. I would work the camp/program, and then I would take the girls back to where they lived and work my extra hours. For two weeks straight, I worked about one hundred and sixty hours.

It took such a toll on me that my heart wasn't functioning properly. But after a situation occurred, which I allowed one of the youths to plug in his radio, which I assumed went against policy, and she no longer wanted me there.

There wasn't a thank you for the job done, yet other staff and youth saw my dedication and learned from what I did. During the times we had staff meetings, two ladies hired after I was, were commended for doing such a great job with the program. But neither her nor my supervisor acknowledged the accomplishments that I had made.

It hurt, but I learned, and was informed that when things were right with her, she was fine. But if you did one thing wrong, not only would you get reprimanded for it, but if there was anything else she wasn't pleased with, you would be reprimanded for them as well and it didn't matter if you had anything to do with it.

Well, I experienced that I had feelings to work through. (*This rose had to fight feelings*). Although I was putting up with things from the youth, their negative attitude and behavior, and even times when they would talk with the owner on the telephone, get off the phone and would laugh in my face and say; "*She didn't get on me for doing that, she understands me*." This would make me and other staff feel as though we had no one to back us up.

It was according to what the youth would say (*This rose was facing tremendous heat from the storm*).

My place of employment was one that was really challenging (*God really kept this rose together*). If one did not have the Lord on his/her side, there would be no way to make it there; because you really had to pray and seek God to come into an environment such as it was.

Although they confessed being a Christian, it would make you question what Christianity really was. Even in all of this, I really enjoyed working with the youth.

When I first started working at the girl's house, I would always make them this corn bread. When I left and went to another house, I would do the same, make them my signature cornbread. And it seemed that wherever I went to make this cornbread, the kids really loved it. And whenever I went to another house and the kids there learned about it, they would get upset. It got to the point that I would show some of them how I made it. But it never took the place of mine. Again, it was my "specialty cornbread".

One of the case managers came into one of the programs where I was working and inquired about it and I told her, it's just normal cornbread.

She stated. "But you make your cornbread with love, and that's why it's so special.

I loved what I did so much working with the youth, yet, I continued to get transferred from one place to the other until I was frustrated.

I contacted the human resource department, and informed them that I needed to be in a stable place with 40 hours.

During this time, I was working in the independent living program with 2 males, ages 18 and 19. The Independent Living Program was a beautiful home, but I was only working 3 hours a day for 7 days. I informed human resource that it was taking 3 weeks of my gas to make up for only one-week worth of a normal work week. This is when she put me in one of the houses that I had worked in the past and was only around the corner from where I lived. The hours I was putting in was taking so much time from my dog. A Maltese. I had to look for a good home for him because I didn't have anyone to watch him while I was working.

My hours were long, but it just wasn't working out for me to keep him. Well, I found a home for him, which I thought was a good home. It was with a grandmother of one of my clients. When I gave her the dog, at first things were fine until one day I got a call from the veterinarian.

I was informed that a female found the dog wondering the streets and took him to a shelter. At the time it saddened me because I thought she really wanted to keep him, but it wasn't a good home. I didn't hear anything else about the dog, just hoped and prayed that they found a good home for him. This was the first time I ever had and owned a dog for over a year.

It was also during this time that I got my own apartment. Things were going really slow for me, but I felt the need to get my own place. I thank God for my sister, and appreciated her for allowing me to live with her the time I did, but I needed my own.

At first, it seemed like a decent place to live. But during the course of looking and then moving in, a spirit of confusion had really attacked me. I was feeling so unsure about the things I wanted and the things I needed (*the confused rose*). During this time, the one thing I learned is that one is experiencing any kind of confusion, do not try to make any decisions.

Well, I moved in, having a peace to pray and a place to call my own. Although at the time, I didn't have any furniture and was sleeping on the floor. A friend of mine from New Jersey was expected to visit, but things were so different. He had mentioned of going to a family reunion.

His sister and her husband were coming to Atlanta, Georgia for a week and I felt that he wanted his sister to meet me, but that wasn't what God wanted.

Things didn't work out for us to meet, or for us to do lunch. Although he was a very nice gentleman and he was single, never married, nor had any children, for some reason, as I explained to him, I didn't want to continue to meet with him. He knew how I felt about him. Yet, he loved his single life and I no longer wanted that, and wanted something more meaningful.

I respected the idea that he wanted to be single, but he had to respect my concern as well. I didn't want him to continue to spend money on me. Although we had great times together (going to the beach, sightseeing, touring areas, laughing and really enjoying each other's company), he didn't want to take it any further and I respected that.

I had to come to the conclusion that I had to stop spending time with him. I was fighting my feelings but feeling hurt along with it. I didn't want to lose our friendship because we had known each other for so long. But I had to make a choice. I didn't want to ruin his choice for not wanting the same thing I did, but on the other hand, I didn't want to be hurt anymore for my decision. So, I stopped calling him and he stopped calling me.

I would have dreams about him that he would just show up at areas where I was, and he would be standing afar off just staring. At times he would be angry or he would have a drink in his hand. This was strange because I had never seen him drink in all of the years I had known him. There were times I would just cry because my feelings were so strong towards him and he knew that. It got to the point when the thoughts of him would come to mind, I would do things to dismiss what I felt, or do something to get my mind off of him. When I moved into my apartment, I would not let him know because of so much pain.

Don't get me wrong, every time we were on the phone, we would be on for 3 or more hours, laughing or soaking up wisdom from each other. It was the same when we were in person.

But strangely, all of that seemed to change the last time. I prayed that God would take the feelings I had towards him away. He did at that time, but for some reason we would not talk for a year or so, and would always start back talking again. He would always say that I pull wisdom out of him because I would question whatever he tells me. He knew a lot about life through his traveling.

It was also during this time that my 15 year-old grandson was going to visit my sister in Virginia and wanted me to meet him there.

He felt that he had not seen me in about 2 years but it wasn't quite that long. But to him it seemed to be longer to a degree (*this rose is fighting through emotional barriers).*

Arrangements were made for me to go. But I wanted someone to ride with me. But the person I asked to go changed her mind at the last minute So, I decided to go alone. I never drove that far alone before. So, I prayed and went. The Lord took me there safely. When I pulled up, he saw my car and came outside to greet me, hugging me before I could get out. He couldn't tell me enough how much he misses me and wish I would move back to New Jersey.

One day he wanted to go to my sister's grandchild's ballgame, but he didn't want me to be left at the house alone. Although he left to go with her, a short time after leaving I heard the door open. He had my sister bring him back to the house because he didn't want me to be alone. During my time there, he and I laughed so hard, watched movies together and played game after game after game of ping pong. And he beat me in every game. I think we played over 100 games. But it was just the time he wanted me to spend with him. The night before I got ready to leave, he kept crying and slept on the floor next to my bed. The next morning when I woke up, and was getting ready to leave, he again didn't want me to go.

To prolong my leaving, I just stayed there standing around talking to my sister and my grandson. He kept wiping his eyes. My sister asked him what was wrong. He said, "The wind got in my eyes." We found out that he was crying and that it wasn't the wind at all. He asked if I could stay longer to go to Texas with them the next day, but I had explain to him that I couldn't. Instead, what I would do is make more arrangements to come back to Virginia to meet him.

As I was leaving out of the house, it was so hard, because I really enjoyed spending time with my grandson. I love all of my grandchildren, but he was the one that kept wanting to be around me and wanted me to return back to New Jersey.

Upon returning to Georgia, I stopped a few times to think of my visit with my sister and my grandchild. When I got back to Georgia, I told my younger sister all of what I had experienced, the time spent with my grandson and how his response to me while there. It will certainly be one to remember. He was the only grandchild that when he was born, he and his mother lived with me. There were times when I would come home from work, he would crawl across his mom to lay on my chest and fall asleep. He and I had developed an un-breakable bond from that point on.

Chapter two

"Another Change"

Memories of what had been happening to me have brought about a much, changed individual. I feel much rejection, more than usual. Sometimes I tell people that when we go through trials, we still have to hold on to God's hands. We know that His word says that He will not allow anyone to pluck us out of His hands. Although tests may come and also trials may come, He still won't let them overtake us. He will not allow us to go under. Yes, we may have to cry sometimes. Yes, we may have to walk alone sometimes, not just sometimes, but many times. Yes, we may have to grieve sometimes, but through it all, we are not alone (*this rose was feeling much rejection*).

I moved back to New Jersey in 2016. First moving in with my daughter, then moving into my own apartment three months later. I tell people that "*God Set Me Up.*" I can laugh about it now, but after realizing what was happening, I really wanted to remain in Georgia. I say that because it was during the time I was working at a hospital in Georgia, and I kept getting phone calls. During this time, I had written a couple books and the personnel from there had brought some of them and encouraged me to write the second part of one of them.

Some directors, doctors and nurses would tell me that, "people all of the time would speak of writing a book, but they never did. But you did it." Nevertheless, it was during this time, that I was told that my oldest son was having a major surgery, my daughter had a minor surgery, my daughter-in-law was having complications with her pregnancy as well as my oldest granddaughter having complications with hers. I made up my mind than that I need to go back to New Jersey. I sold my mobile home and moved back, with the help of my middle son. When I got back, I felt that I was needed in each situation; through prayers and helping in whatever way I could.

But the fact was, that I had to go back to finish Pastoring. God had opened doors for me to do Women's Conferences, Revivals and other Domestic Violence events. But the Pastoring, I felt I had to complete the work that I had once ran away from because of much devastation, hurt and pain I had endured. Sometimes when a person is dealing with pain, they do and say things that they normally would not. (*This rose was struggling with pain*).I went to Pastoring and have been ever since.

There were times I would see people that had known me for years and would call me by my first name, which was okay. But God let me know that in many of these cases, they did it to try and demean me or not give me the respect that was due to me.

Not because I was such a great person, or the fact that I was Pastoring, but for the cause of God calling me into Pastoring. Now I look and see that it wasn't my ignorance, but theirs. No, I don't do as other Pastors, but I do as I'm led by God. But one thing He let me know, and that was to know who I am. He had called me from birth to Pastor, that was why I was so different than the people I hung around; and to those who thought that they knew me, I was a total stranger. At first, that used to bother me, but God had to quickly remind me. *"I CREATED YOU FOR MY GLORY."*

He also let me know, to show those same ones disrespecting me, "love", continue to be who I am and keep it moving. Sometimes we get upset at God because He doesn't move the way we expect Him to. But He said in *Isaiah 55:8-9, "For my thoughts are not your thoughts, neither are your ways my ways, saith the LORD. For as the heavens are higher than the earth, so are my ways higher than your ways, and my thoughts than your thoughts."*

We want God to move on our time. But, one thing about God, is that He sees us for who we are and moves on His own timing. If God were to move on our timing, almost everyone would be destroyed. That's just how ugly our ways are to Him. God is a Mighty God and does things as He sees fit to do *(This rose had to be humbled).*

I was in my apartment now for almost a year when one of my older sisters passed. It was somewhat hard, but God really helped me through it. It was on me to take her to church the week prior to her passing. During this time, she was in a nursing home because she had been in a coma for a while.

During her time in a coma, the doctors told the family to come together because her heart was getting weaker and so on. But one of my sisters overheard a doctor say that one of the medications she was on was causing her heartbeat to slow down. After she told the doctor what she heard, he tried to recant what he said. (*But one of the things I found out, that when a person is hospitalized, that family need to make as many visits with them as possible. All doctors aren't bad, but there are some who are just doing it for the paycheck; like a lot of people are doing now, not only the doctors. Because a person is working a professional job, doesn't mean that they are doing it for the best interest of the patients*).

After that, they withdrew that medication from her, and she came out of the coma and she remembered those that visited her. They, at first transferred her to another hospital, then after that to a nursing home. I don't think she was in the nursing home a month before she had passed. I had mentioned earlier that I took her to church. She used to love going to church and singing on the choir.

When I took her that Sunday, the choir dedicated a beautiful song to her. She stood up and began singing word for word that song. Everyone was so proud of her. After church service, we went out to eat then I returned her back to the nursing home. I don't think she lived a week after that. But I was so thankful to have spent time with her.

It was a week after her funeral when I got a visit from my nephew whom I had raised after his mother was murdered. When he came to visit me, I was so happy to see him, because I had not seen him in over 10 years. When I saw him, he still had that smile that said; "I am glad to see you." We spoke for a while and for some reason, a relief came over me. I now had a peace because I realize that he was okay. It was strange because me seeing him, although it brought relief, also brought tears. Meaning that all of a sudden, I began to grieve his mother's death after 24 years, as well as my sister's death who had just past about over a week ago. When he got home, he called me back. *(He calls me mom sometimes, because I was the only mother he knew after his mother was murdered).*

He asked me, "Mom, are you okay? Did my dad do or say anything to you?" If so, I'm going to do this and that.... I told him no! I didn't want him to do anything to hurt anyone.

He said to me, "Remember when I was a child that you told me that if I ever needed a shoulder to cry on that your shoulder was there for me? Well, now I'm telling you. If you ever need a shoulder to cry on, mine is here for you!" The tears really began to flow then, because I thought that he forgot about the things I had told him. It was then, when I saw him and knowing that he was alright that I began to grieve his mother (my sister's) death like I had mentioned earlier.

It was delayed grief and I started really going through. It was in November of 1993 that his mother was murdered and he had witnessed it. He first witnessed his father beating his mother on many occasions. Then, at the age of 2 & 1/2 that he witnessed his father stabbing her to death in front of him and his niece. But a month prior to that, God had spoken to me, letting me know that I may have to raise him. It was during the time I was babysitting him and we were on our way to the school to vote, that God spoke that to me. When He did, I stopped in my tracks, looked at him and said, "Nah, nothing is going to happen to (my sister). God had also showed me in a vision that the funeral procession was going to leave from my apartment; and had showed me talking about it in a store that was down the street from where I lived.

The night it happened, everything God showed me happened, exactly the way He showed it to me. I didn't quite understand it when He showed it to me, but after it happened, everything came back to me. That same night they brought my nephew to my apartment. When I began raising him, I remember he and I were in the kitchen of my apartment. I was cooking him breakfast when I heard him say, "Yes mom, I'm happy here!" I turned around and asked him who was he talking too? He said, "My mom. She asked me if I was happy here!" I knew that God does mysterious things, but I had never seen Him do this.

He then began going through behaviors that were so negative. Because of what he had witnessed, I could not use a knife in front of him; every siren he heard affected him and every yellow ribbon he saw made him go into rages of anger; this was because he never forgot about the things he witnessed the night she was murdered. It was a heart-wrenching situation for me because he was still a baby! But this was a situation that changed my entire life. It was also during this time the local newspaper had written an article about a daycare and had his picture in the paper. This bothered me.

I had also written a couple articles about domestic violence in the newspaper and when I would see different people on the streets, they would ask me; "When will the next article come out?"

"Another Change"

I stopped writing because some people had the wrong mind-set of what I was doing. It was during this time that I realized that I had to make a change. After-a-while I began moving from that particular apartment to a mobile home not far, then moved into an entirely different area. I was changing schools because one school in Willingboro began victimizing him again, and the things that were happening to him began to become a domino effect.

After sharing with them what he had experienced just in case he had an outburst, they took that and turned it around on him. And through all of that, he had become a victim of society. He had so much anger in him. But I told him that I would be there for him. In which I tried to do, but was hindered. But it was because of all of what I went through that brought me to this point. I thought that I had already grieved my sister's death, because whenever he cried, I cried. And that was the only time God would allow me to cry concerning her.

Now, it was after all of those years that my behavior changed. I started having attitudes, crying a lot and acting in ways that weren't like me *(This rose was withered with pain.)*

I was off work for about a couple weeks. *(This rose didn't think she was going to make it through the storm).*

I remember going to work that following week. My supervisor and the manager of the program told me that I needed to talk to someone. At first, they recommended that I see a counselor from their company to talk to. I was informed that the first three visits were free. But if I needed counseling afterwards, that I had to pay.

In the beginning, I was hesitant. But then realizing that I really did need to talk to someone, I remember making the appointment.

When I went to the appointment, she just asked what was happening with me? I started talking and talking and talking. She recommended that I write down my feelings; I told her I already did; then she recommended other things to do. Whatever she recommended, I had already done. She had no words for me other than, "Well, you've already done everything; there is nothing else I can tell you." She didn't know what else to do. She just looked and shrugged her shoulders. She said that I could make another appointment, and I looked at her.

My thoughts were, if you could not help me process the things that I am dealing with on my first appointment, or make any suggestions, why should I come back? I explained that I won't need another appointment. There was absolutely nothing that she did that led me to believe she could help me.

Upon returning back to work, they could not ask me what our discussions were. But one thing, it did not change what I was dealing with. Both my supervisor and the manager of the program suggested that I needed to take time off, and as much time that I needed. I then called my sister in Virginia and asked to go there. I was there for two weeks. But upon the time I arrived the Lord led me to stay in the bedroom until after twelve noon. I remember my brother-in-law coming to the door and he stated to my sister that, "she stays in that room." It wasn't until later that I had to tell them why I had to stay in the room.

Every morning they would prepare nice breakfasts, that consists of fried potatoes and onions, bacon, ham, fried apples, grits, buttery biscuits, sausage; you name it, they prepared it. I do remember gaining weight because the lunch and dinner were prepared the same way with heavy meals. It was during my stay in the room that the Lord had me to really cry out to Him. I remember crying so intensely to the point where both of my eyes were so swollen. I cried and cried and cried everyday while there.

I had to just lay before God and release everything within me out. I thought that when it was time for me to leave that I was over it, but I wasn't. I didn't realize that I still had pain to go through.

I returned back home and remembered going to a church service. When the alter call was made, I remembered going to the Alter and kneeled down. I normally don't kneel when going to the Alter. This time I did, and I wept like a baby. I don't know how long I was down there but realized when I got up that I was the only one left at there. I got up and returned to my seat. But it seemed that, the last cry right there at the Altar, made the difference and has been okay ever since.

One thing that did bother me though was when my next to my oldest sister had died prior to going to Virginia It bothered me that no one was there for me. No one called to check on me; no one gave me a card or phone call of concern. No one was there at the funeral for support for me. I felt so deserted. It wasn't until a month later that I got a Sympathy Card from my job.

Then only some employees signed. When I returned, I found out that everyone didn't know about my sister's death. We were a small program with roughly around fourteen employees. But hardly anyone knew about my sister's death except for the day staff, which was about seven employees.

Some evening or night staff knew of her death and a couple day staff didn't. My thoughts on that wasn't good at all. What would it have hurt to receive a phone call or some kind of concern or support? I did receive a signed card from some of the employees. My concern was how can you work for a domestic violence shelter and not have a caring heart. That right there let me know that I did not need to be there *(One of this rose's pedals were crushed).*

Chapter Three

"The Challenge"

It's been now almost a couple of years and God is still moving in my life. One of my sisters had gone to Virginia with me one of the times that I had an assignment to preach. She gave her heart to God and began to really cry out to Him. Upon Pastoring, she is now one of my members and God is really helping her through the process. This particular sister is next to my younger sister and was a fighter, curser, you name it. Now, God is doing a work in her. She is now helping with the church, and my domestic violence events. I thank God for her.

Back in 2009 I started a Domestic Violence Walk & Rally in New Jersey. I left the state after a year because I was dealing with pain and hurt from being abused. It was during that time I moved to Florida, then to Georgia, like I had mentioned earlier. Upon returning to New Jersey, I started the walk back again, but left from doing that to starting my own business in helping domestic violence victims that are already in a domestic violence shelter or program. Now, every year we raise funds to help victims start their lives over again.

I remember going through in 2018. It was so many difficult trials. Many days I cried. And I mean many days I had to cry.

Many days I felt and was really alone. But every time God brought me through. There were times when I would Minister the word that people were just doing other things. They were reading their Bibles, playing with their phones, talking and walking back and forth. Sometimes I would stop just to see how people would respond. At that point they would look up. I use to ask God, "God am I that boring?" But was informed that it wasn't that I was boring, but the adversary wanted me to believe that people weren't listening to shut me up and sit me down. I had to continue to preach whether I wanted to or not and when I felt like it or not.

It was also those times God would let me know that I was still faithful. It was in being faithful regardless of the testing that He was concerned about. He yet told me as well as others in His word, to be faithful over the few things. It is those times that would determine if Ministry was called to me or if I was called to Minister. When we are called to Minister, we do so even if only one or two were present. We would Minister to those one or two as if the whole house was full of people. But if we just went and weren't called to that position, we would easily give up because of the crowd not being there, if the crowds weren't paying us any attention, or if the money wasn't coming in.

One of the things I found out with ministry is that (I actually saw it on social media) “God doesn’t call those that are equipped, but He equips the called.” Boy, that is a hard pill to swallow. Because those of us that He called, we really don’t want to preach. I know that I am one that didn’t want to. I didn’t want to Pastor, I didn’t want to pray for the sick, I didn’t want to lay hands and I didn’t feel like going out into the cold, wet snowy weather to help bring deliverance to anyone. But because God called me to the Ministry, and it was like a glove that the ball automatically fit, it made me fit right into the right place which He called me *(This rose is in challenging storms).*

So many times we fight to obey God. Not so much that we don’t want to obey Him, but we want to make sure that it is He that is telling us to do certain things. I know for years the Lord would tell me to tell people things and I would hold back because I didn’t want to make a mistake and for people to call me a false Prophet. But when God saw fit that I was ready, it would automatically come out of my mouth. I didn’t have time to decide if I could, should or will or will not. He made sure that I spit it out. I can now laugh at myself because things would come out of my mouth that had people not want to deal with me. And, on the other hand, some would call for me just to Prophesy to them.

I had to tell them that I can't give them something that isn't in me to give. I am not a false Prophet and I am not going to lie to you. If God isn't giving me anything to give you, I am not going to try to make up anything. People stopped asking after that. One thing I said that I will not do, and that is Propha-lie. I just can't do it. Some people Propha-lie out of their own heart, but that's not me. One thing people don't understand is that, every word that comes out of our mouth, whether good, bad, indifferent, or whatever the case may be, that we are going to be held accountable.

Many people today will not deal with me because they can't figure me out. They stay as far away from me as possible. I used to ask different people, "is there a sign on my back that says "Hate Me?" Some laughed when I said that and would ask me, "what do you mean?" I would tell them that I am so despised by so many. Some don't like me and, to keep it real, they themselves don't and can't even tell me why. Some don't like me because some of their friends don't like me. And you know, that is so sad, because to me, if a person can't think for themselves and have to have a friend, family member or foe to dictate to them, they themselves aren't as real as they say that they are. I always tell people, even when I preach, that "the day of judgment, God is not going to ask you anything about me and He is not going to ask me anything about you."

But one thing for sure, He will judge you for how you treated me, and He will judge me for how I treat you. It is a shame now-a-days that people don't have to have a reason to dislike you, they dislike you just because of who you are. I am reminded so many times that the way to destruction is wide and many there will be able to find it. But the way to heaven is narrow and few there be that will follow that road.

There are so many people that really don't want to live righteous anymore. Many feel that if they compromise with the world that they will be better accepted. But if being accepted by what other people do and how they feel change me, they aren't worth being in my life. I do not and will not allow people to determine if I go to heaven or hell. Neither will I pay attention to that sympathy role that if I don't do this or that, that I am not a true Christian. Well, I am a true Christian if I play it, but still will not play both fields. I do not want to fall into the hands of God being angry with me, just because of someone else. *(This rose has a defense).*

Chapter Four

"A Bruising Process"

I began experiencing some difficulty with my feelings after going through a very hard trial of a type of harassment situation. I began crying, feeling exposed to shame, hurt, humiliation and anger. Not all of the time knowing how to manage or handle my feelings but trying to maintain them the best way I knew how.

Every time I went out my door, going out and coming in, I would always look behind me. I also began looking into the laundry room and other doors when I went by them; not knowing if I would see the person that caused my emotional pain. I also got phone calls from the people in the area that I knew. But because of what I experienced, I didn't know if they knew the person and would call because of them. It had gotten to the point where I had to get help by seeing a psychologist. I would cry, feeling scared and I was an emotional wreck. Although I would never ask the person, I would wait to see if they gave themselves away. But through it all, I maintained a very protective composure. It was for myself, not for anyone else. I needed that to protect myself. I've never gone through such an emotional state such as that. God had to really keep me. I forgot who I was and had to get help because I was traumatized by the situation.

No one could understand what I was going through, and I had only shared the situation with only a few people outside of my children. When I told my children, some cried and the other wanted to harm the person. I told them that God would deal with them, that it wasn't for them to get involved. God saw the situation and God will be the one to handle it. I know He will, because He let me know that. But the fact of me having to go through it was very hard. *(This rose went through an emotional bruising process).*

I had to speak at an event I was hosting and wanted to cancel, but after the advertisement was out, I couldn't back down. But I remember fumbling over my words and doing everything I could to not mention that what I was speaking about, I recently went through the ordeal myself. But I had to learn how to be strong. Although sometimes being strong for others is one thing but trying to be and remain strong for yourself is something altogether different. Feeling numb while being strong is hard to shuffle. Knowing that some of my grandchildren were at the event and people that I knew personally, I had to try to keep it together as much as I could. It was very hard for me, but God took me through it.

Being strong isn't always easy. Sometimes you feel as if you are going to lose it.

With a feeling of shame and hurt, we can at times all of a sudden begin to feel old; don't feel like ourselves; we don't want to look like the pain we are dealing with, but for some odd reason we can feel weighted down with the hurt. At times, we can't even explain it. We don't want to feel rejected, and cast others aside for fear that they will reject you who you are.

Not that you want to hurt others, but when someone disappoints you, you automatically take on a rejection stage. And during the event on Saturday, March 23, 2019, I felt so much rejection, pain, guilt, sorrow, embarrassment, and anger to the point where others had to console me. That day was a day where I asked myself the question; Who is really for me? The looks I witnessed of some not wanting to be there, but was there because they had already purchased a ticket, gave me another feeling of rejection. Sometimes when you look at faces and see things, it sometimes makes you feel like what is the use, is it worth it? Should I just stop what I am doing?

Should I cancel future events? All of these mixed emotions had entered my mind. They enter your mind when you're already dealing with circumstances and you feel that if one more thing is added on this plate, I'll lose it! But, of course, that's flesh talking. God is a keeper and He will keep you, if, in your heart you really want to be kept.

I want to be kept. I want to continue to have my events. It's just the fact where I have to trust God through the process. *(This rose had a trusting issue).*

Then the next day you see people who normally don't smile with you, you witnessed them now laughing in your face because knowing that your event was a failure and they were part of the reason that it was. It was so strange how you try to support people when you can, but the same people not knowing your situation have attitudes toward you because of what other people are saying. Your trust level will begin to flop.

But I know that God has everything in control. Sometimes with that you have to realize that it isn't my turn yet. Which is all good. I do know that God sees and knows all of what happened. He also sees the ones that have been coming against me and trying all they can to hinder what He placed for my hands to do. But one thing came to mind? I'm thinking that it was failure, but God doesn't fail us; but it was only a lesson, not a failure. But on the other hand, I learned that several funerals were taking place that day as well. There will always be a next time. But the love I have for people will remain. Because if those same people need a slice of bread, or water in order to survive, I will be right there for them.

So, it's not only me that goes through this, but those that are called by the name of the Lord who have a calling on their lives. Love last longer than hate! So, I have to keep on loving, Amen? *(Boy, this rose is learning lessons to keep her pedals afloat).*

Chapter Five

"Defending What God Says"

I was talking about backing off of people because of their behaviors and attitudes. Since then, I've learned to deal with who I am first. My priority is learning to accept me for who I am, not for what others think of me. One of the areas I have and still am learning, is that dealing with my children hasn't always been a bed of roses. I used to feel like there were no manuals to learn on how to be a good Mother, or even a parent. I did whatever I thought was right to do. I never had a relative to tell me or even explain to me how to be a parent or tell me what to do as a parent; other than to beat my child when they were bad or acting out. And in being a single parent, I had to learn the best way I could.

There were many days we were low on food, but God always made a way for us. When I returned to New Jersey from living in Florida and Georgia, at first my children were happy to see me. Then that wore off after a while. I felt many days like picking myself up again and leaving. Thinking, maybe they would appreciate me more if I wasn't around them and that they wouldn't have so easy access to me. That maybe then, they would appreciate me. These were only some of the things I experienced.

I went through a phase where I thought that my children hated me. They would not call me, check up on me nor be there when I needed them. They were always in their own world, doing them! Sometimes I would text or call and would not get a response for days at a time. Sometimes I wouldn't get response at all. I felt that I was in a world all by myself. I felt lonely, neglected and disliked by my own children.

But people on the outside would look at it and say, "Your children are so respectful". They didn't know that the rose was fighting hard just to survive its feelings. They could not understand the pressure I was dealing with. All they saw was respect from my children. Don't get me wrong; I thank God that I was able to raise them in that manner. So many children today do not have that respect for their parents, grandparents or anyone. I thank God for that. I love my children and admire who they have become. But sometimes a parent at times need to hear from them. Even if it's just them saying, "Mom, I appreciate you."

On another note, It had been a week of experiences in dealing with family. My youngest son had gone through an ordeal with people following him, breaking into his home, doing things to his cars in the driveway of his home and flattening his tires.

While sitting on his back step at night, lights shining on him, cars racing in front of his home at 3 and 4 in the mornings. His concern was, who can he go to, to report what he's dealing with? They were even taking pictures of him while driving.

My mind goes back to one evening I went to a church to have prayer. It was around 6 in the evening when I got down to pray, the Lord dealt with me to go to my son's house and pray around it. I was saying to myself at first that I'll go when I get done praying. But I could not get into prayer because the Lord dealt with me even stronger to get up and go to his house.

When I got up, I drove to his home. Upon my arrival, he came outside to greet me. But one thing I had noticed was two vehicles was next door with their parking lights on. Then a third vehicle pulled up. But when I got out of my car, I started going around his home, praying in the Spirit out loud. I began to bind up Satan and his imps, praying that *"No weapon formed against him (and his household) was going to prosper and that every tongue that rose up against him in judgment, shall be condemned." Isaiah 54:17.*

That anyone that is fighting against him and his household that God was going to fight against theirs, this prayer continued on for about an hour.

I continued to walk around the horseshoe of his driveway, continuing to pray aloud and some in tongues. I did not care who heard, neither did I feel fearful. All I knew that God sent me there on a mission and I had to follow His lead. After a while, the cars started leaving. I felt in my Spirit that the people in those cars had planned on doing something to my son that night. But God blocked it. *(This rose is still standing through the storm).* My son said to me, "Mom, thank you because I know that God sent you here. Normally, my wife or some of her children would be here during this time. But for some reason, she and all of the children left." I know that was nobody but God! God will protect His children from harm's way. I am a witness to this. Regardless of the situation, He will be there. He said, *"The effectual prayer of the righteous man availeth much." James 5:16*

And, although there were many things that were happening to his home, I was going through with mine own apartment as well as people coming into my own apartment, leaving my personal information out on my nightstand; seasoning left on my countertops and stove, my underwear drawer gone through, with my drawers left open. My clothes missing, my leather coat with a hole in it, my electric stove on, upon returning home from work 12:45 am, knowing that I left home around 2pm to go to work and didn't return until 12:45 am.

(This rose needs to be watered with understanding, withering but yet growing at the same time). How can one explain this? No one in the building seemed to know anything.

Still, who do I put a complaint on? Do I sign a complaint on the entire company where I live? Another time I misplaced something inside of my apartment; at least I thought I misplaced it. It happened to show up after an inspection, in my utensil drawer. Wow! What a coincident! Some information was erased from it; what in the world are you looking for? *(But the things this rose had to encounter; withering, but still standing)!*

One day I was in prayer about what was happening in my apartment, but God reminded me, that although people are coming in and out of my apartment, they cannot destroy me because He has my back. *(Lord, refresh this rose!).* He has and is still keeping me. He lets me know *that "No man can pluck me out of His hands."*

This is only some of the things I had to endure while living in the apartment building. But I can say, that I really thank God for being a keeper of my soul and a keeper of my mind. And some of the events I was having, I really felt that some of the people in the building were being paid or given favors to try and destroy me or my reputation.

One thing about God, that some people fail to realize, is that, if God is for you, the whole world is against you. And rather they SAY that they are Christians or non-Christians, both will get the same judgment as to dealing with God's people. Because now they have allowed Satan to represent who they are. I look at them and smile, knowing that God said that vengeance belongs to Him. And just like He let me know, that their days are numbered. Regardless of who they are and what title or position they hold. That gives me reassurance that there is no need to fight in this battle because this battle is the Lords'. But this isn't just for me; it is also for the ones' that reading this book. You too have no need to fight in these battles, because God has your back. Don't become spiteful nor vengeful.

Then my oldest son had started going through things in his life. He had been shot at many times, been hit by more than several vehicles. Then going to the doctor to get medication to help him with pain, he became addicted to pain killers. One time in particular, he told me that he went to a rehab to see a friend of his. His friend was released from the hospital and had to start walking all over again. So, upon him leaving the rehab, a van hit him and it threw him into some bushes. The van went up the street and turned around, coming back toward him again, attempting to hit him. He then jumped out of the way and hit his head.

During this time, other vehicles witnessed it and stopped to help him, but the van spun away. He was hit a couple more times. I had been telling him to go to the hospital, but he refused. I remember other times he would call me telling me that some people had contracts out on him, thinking he was someone else, but just because he hung with different people, they thought he had something to do with some things they did. I remember praying. Thank God, He blocked those contracts and he was able to go to those people to explain that it wasn't him. *(This rose has gone through much turmoil, but still standing).* He had been shot at, but the bullet that was meant for him, hit the person behind him.

One day he overdosed while trying to get his blood sugar down. I was informed that when it occurred that he had passed out and a friend of his found him. He had died for about 5 to 10 minutes and a friend and his son had resuscitated him. The ambulance was called, and he was admitted to the hospital. Prior to him being admitted, when I got the information from my daughter, I went to the hospital to see him. He was alert and had told me what had happened. He said that he had received his prescription from the pharmacy. His blood sugar was low, so he gave himself 5 units of insulin.

The insulin didn't work so he injected 10 more units, along with other pain killers and other medication. His youngest son was one of the ones that found him, and he was screaming and yelling to have seen his father in that condition. When my son was telling me that, he broke down crying stating and it hurt me to see my son like that. Then he asked if I could go home to get some personal items. I didn't want to, but I forgot to pick it up anyways. When I returned, his sister and half-sister, his daughter and his friend were there. I didn't stay long because I was already tired from dealing with other issues this week. *(This rose is withering again from the storms)!*

The next day he texted me asking if I could bring his phone charger and his children up to see him. At this time, my body was too tired to move. I told him that I could not because I was too tired to get up. *(Right now, this rose needed refreshing).*

He later texted me telling me to take care of myself. That was something I had to do without being told. When my body gets like that, it is frightening to me and I know that my body will eventually shut down. The following day I did go up to see him. He was alright at first, then he was beginning to get a little jittery. When I went up there, there was a female in the room monitoring him.

My son had been put on suicide watch because of overdosing on medication and pills. The agency came in regarding the children and I was informed of them may having to remove the children. I told the nurse that he has enough family to help with his children and I was not going to let the agency put those children in foster care because they had already gone through enough. They didn't need any more trauma in their lives. Two people had come into his room to talk to him and told me I had to leave. I informed them that I was his mother; but was told that he was of age and they had to talk to him alone. When they left, he was upset. He stated that the agency will be coming up there to talk to him about his children. I was already tired, so I left.

Later that night he called me telling me to come pick him up because he was leaving the hospital. I told him that I was not coming to pick him up and he is going to stay there and get the right help that he needs. He was going through a withdrawal stage and was crying, upset, stating that he was sweating and that the nurses would not give him anything for his problem. For over a half an hour I was praying with him, reading scriptures to him and having him repeat the scriptures while reading them.

After while he said that he could not take any more of it. I then hung up and called the nurse's station.

I was informed that while speaking to them, a nurse was already in his room to give him the medication he needed. I thanked the nurse. I then hung up. It took so much out of me. *(There again, that rose is being hit with different types of trauma from different angles).*

As a parent, that moment was so hard and challenging for me. It hurt in one way because I could not do anything else but pray and read the word of God; on the other hand, I was thankful that he was getting the help he needed.

Chapter Six

"Traumatizing Situations"

After my son was released from the hospital, not long, the agency came to see the children. They wanted to do contracts for him, that the children would not be left alone with him. His eldest daughter and I did the contract at first, but neither of us were able to continue due to our work schedules. I had already informed the agency that I help him with the children, especially as a grandparent.

It was a week from that day he was admitted that I received a phone call that his brother-in-law that he was close with had passed. It was very hard, and traumatizing for him and myself, because his brother-in-law and I would always talk about the Bible. When my son told me that he had recently spoken with him, it upset him the more. My son stated that when he spoke to him on the phone, he told him that he was getting ready to take a nap and would reach out to him when he woke up.

My son informed me that he never woke up and his wife had found him. He was devastated because the both of them always were together. His brother-in-law was over to his house quite a bit. When I would go to my son's house and if he was there, the both of us would get into a discussion about the Bible.

It would be very interesting, because there were times I had to leave, and he would walk me to the door and didn't want to end the conversation. My son would have to always tell him, "man, my mom has to leave, she has to go to work."

It was during that week that I was able to contact his wife to give her my condolence. When I did, it was during the time when I was at work and I had to step out of the office into the hallway. The both of us wept and I could actually feel her pain. I prayed with her, and she asked if I could continue to keep her in my prayers. I finally hung up, but it was like a cloud over me because he was more like a son to me. He was always taking care of his children and would teach them the skills that he learned. He also would spend time with my son's children like they were his own. Helping them with their homework, buying things for them like his own and doing his best to teach them how to clean a house.

During the time of his funeral it was somewhat hard for me, but especially for my children. My daughter could not handle being there and although my two sons attended, it was hard for the both of them to a degree. I didn't think my oldest son was going to attend because the last funeral he attended, was at his father's. Although he attended, he handled himself really well.

After the funeral his wife asked me to not stop staying in contact with her. I promised her that I would not. I did stay in contact with her after the funeral for a while.

April 2019

Going into the month of April, it seemed that this year is going by really fast. It started off by having an appointment with a therapist. It brought back tears, pain and hurt. The hurt reflected of something that had occurred to me. Sometimes people may look at you and think that they may know exactly what a person is dealing with. But they have no idea what's really going on inside of a person's heart.

We, as people know how to camouflage a smile. We can be hurting on the inside and yet, torn. But once we leave our company, or those we are trying not to hurt in front of, we release all of the tears, hurt, etc. But sometimes others can see through to our pain. There are times of the ones that can see our pain that they either try to encourage, or talk about you to others or even laugh at you in the face.

In their mind they assume that it doesn't take all of that, but yet, not knowing the truth behind a matter, their judgement is wrong and is totally off. I look at people sometimes and I pay attention to how they respond to things.

What I see at times leave me wondering if they really have a clue what others have observed, or are they are going by what someone else says about the matter. *(This rose is rising in alertness).*

One thing I saw starting off this month is how people will try to manipulate a person and want to take matters into their own hands. God told me to take my control back. *(This rose is fighting back).*

I allowed certain people, places and things to take control over what I do and who I am. I had to put a stop to that. It also let me see how a person can take over and control a person that is hurting. It's not that they are concerned about the person or situation, but they look at the situation as if that's their time to control the environment. What I see with that is a spirit of manipulation and dominating, which also leads to a spirit of witchcraft or a jezebel spirit.

Dealing with people in my past would give me pointers on how witches function. No, not that I have ever wanted to be one or do things to hurt, harm or control anyone; but the fact is why and how they operate. I was told that this is what witches do and the jezebel spirit of how they operate. I have learned and have been taught that you don't kick a person while they are down, but help them to get up, or move out of the way to allow them space to get up *(This rose was traumatized).*

Chapter Seven

"Lessons I had to Learn"

Going back to my son's situation, I received a call from him asking if I could come and pick him up because he had been shot and his house was shot up as well. I told him that I could not because God told me to not to leave out of my house. He could not understand that because he felt that I should have come to his rescue. As a parent I really wanted to, but it was only a couple days prior to that where I had a vision. In this vision, I saw a funeral car and funeral flowers in front of my apartment building. I didn't know if I should have gone to get him, or if the person or persons that were after him, would follow me to do me any harm. *(The rose is doing some withering from the storms)*

My son was really upset with me about that. But I had to continue to explain to him why I could not come. He had informed me that his youngest son had just gotten up off the couch when a bullet came through the wall and pierced the wall in the living room where my grandson (his son) was sitting. His oldest daughter had just dropped him off when the situation occurred, and she took the children with her. I know that it had to have been God with them at the time. I did not want to interrupt what was happening and putting myself in harm's way.

When my son finally spoke to me, he stated that he slept down to my sister's the next night. I guess some looked at me as being a bad parent for what I did, but I had to obey God. At this point, I did not have time to worry about what other people felt about my decision. I had to think of my safety. *(This rose is still fighting, even harder now)*

God had already told me on several occasions that he has my children in his care and told me not to worry about them. I had to come to the conclusion to take him at His Word and trust His decision; especially concerning this situation. Was it hard for me to do? Yes! But I had to trust what He told me.

It was weeks following the situation where the agency no longer wanted the children in the same household as my son because they felt the children's lives was in danger. My son had to finally go to court. He asked if I could take him. I told him that I would, but I could no longer be on the contract because what he was going through was beginning to be too hard for me to handle, and it was affecting my health. My other children were upset with me for getting involved because they said that I was getting too old and it wasn't my responsibility. My daughter stated that she would help out instead of me since she is much younger, and I should be somewhere enjoying my life. So, I gave them her information.

When it was time for court, I knew that the agency really wanted the children in foster care, but God had another plan. When my son was in court that morning, the worker came to get the both of us. The judge presiding told us to come back in the afternoon. When my son and I went outside, the worker was outside and asked him a question that he refused to adhere to. So, she stated, "Are you refusing?" And he said, yes. At first it made me upset and I told him that he had to find another way to court in the afternoon. That is how bad it had affected me, and it made me angry.

The word of God says in Ephesians *4:26(a) "Be ye angry, and sin not..."* I had to realize how angry I was and get a hold of myself. But after lying down and thinking matters over, I called to see if he had another way to court. He said, No, that he had already called to cancel. I told him that I would take him, but he had to find another way back home because I had to meet someone in the area and could not bring him back home.

The next day in speaking with him, he told me that the judge ruled in his favor. That the judge got in the worker's case and favored him. I told him that he should know that God was on his side and the favor from the judge was God working on his behalf. He understood that and was very thankful *(This rose learned a valuable lesson).*

It was that Sunday when I picked him up for church that he walked the floor giving God the praise and Glory that belonged to him. My sister, my son's friend and another male friend of theirs also attended service. The other male that came, gave his life to Jesus. That was a new beginning for everyone in there. I saw God's hands at work in the matter. It also encouraged me to stay focused on the plan of God.

Chapter Eight

"A Rightful Praise"

Later that week, I got a text from a co-worker. I didn't at first know which worker it was because when I had to change phones, most of my contacts were lost. So, I did not know who text me. The text stated that my boss had gotten fired. I told the one that text me that she still needed our prayers regardless.

There are times we never know if we have to go through the same situation as others. So, it pays not to point fingers at anyone. For the Word of God says in *Romans 3:23, "For all have sinned and come short of the Glory of God...."*

It was a day or two after that that I contacted our new supervisor. She confirmed her being fired. She also told me other matters of the building as I as well told her some of my concerns. I knew that I would not be there that week because of plans already being in order. That Saturday a friend of mine was coming from another state and I had to meet her and cover her in prayer.

That Sunday, I thought I had to Minister the word, but I was being ordained as a Pastor, under another Pastor. It was an Apostle there also that laid hands on me, as well as the Pastor's mother, who is a great woman of God.

I wept because no one ever ordained me as a Pastor, although I stepped out to be one ordained by God. It was God that dealt with me about Pastoring, but I still needed a covering.

Others wanted me to be under them, but I never felt led. I know that I needed to be under someone who did not compromise the gospel. Not that the others who asked me did not, but I needed to be able to operate under the anointing without the jealousy spirits coming against me. This Pastor who ordained me steps out in the anointing of God. He is no joke and is nothing to play with. I would tell people, if you ever wanted to grow in God, get under this Pastor. I used to help him out years ago in his Ministry, but I left. After reconnecting with him, he reminded me that I was supposed to have been under him all along. I realize now what I needed was a strong leader to be under.

One of the things he made clear was, that he would not stop me from doing what I'm already doing. He would not stop God from working through me. I just needed a covering and at times when he wasn't at his church, he wanted me to be there in his place to act on his behalf. God had already begun setting up things to work in my favor; and to travel. Not that I'm condemning anyone else I just know what I need. I don't need to have anyone finger pointing at me.

And I didn't need anyone trying in any way to compromise what God was doing through me. I also didn't need for anyone to run their mouth about what I went through or even mock what I had to experience in my personal trials.

One of the things I had to come to grips with was that whatever happened, God allowed it. And whatever I had to experience, the first to point a finger was just as much as guilty as I was. Where were they when I needed them? Who and which one made a phone call or even a visit to even pray with me.? NOT A ONE CAME TO LEND A HAND OR A PRAYER! *(This rose was feeling withered).*

When we talk about what the Word of God says, are they doing what the Word of God says to do? Well, let me answer that! No! *St John 8:7 says, "He that is without sin, let him cast the first stone."* Neither person was able to do that, if they say what the Bible really said. Nobody but God knew what I was dealing with.

It had even got to the point where one of the sisters in Christ had a nerve to laugh at me when I spoke to her on the phone about a situation. But what God showed me about her, she should have been the last to want to make any type of comment or laugh at or about anybody. One of the things God showed me was, He had to pull me away from these people because they did not mean me any good.

Yes, just like the Minister had already warned me when I held the Domestic Violence Revival in October of 2017. She said, so many people who I speak with laugh with me in my face and once my back is turned, they talk about me. I know for a fact that it was true because God had already showed me the people that were doing it. Matter of fact, some were at the revival the same night she spoke it. The guilt was all on their face. But I never missed a blink from showing them love anyways.

I just kept matters to myself. Sometimes people think because you're not popular with the cliques that God don't deal with you or you don't know anything. But the God I serve uses whomsoever He will. We, as individuals do not have to justify our calling to anyone. Isn't God just that good? But one thing I did do was I withdrew myself from them. AT first it hurt, but after a while God showed me that where he is taking me, they can't go there. Neither was I going where He was taking them. Not that I think that I am any better than anyone else, I just know and realize what God requires of me.

Walking this walk is a very lonely walk. *(This rose is in the rose garden all alone)* But I rather walk alone then to have snakes, thorns and bristles hindering me.

Don't get me wrong, although I do love all of them, and I really mean that I love them with the love of God, because I could not love them without God. I still have to run on because I got a race to run *(This rose is on a journey).*

Chapter Nine

"The Injustice Role"

It's going into Monday morning.

Good morning everyone! It's now 5:15am. It's good to see another morning. Welcoming another day into my life, it is a blessing. Thinking that today I am going to relax and stay at home, my granddaughter called asking if I could take her to the motor vehicle agency to get her information. She was already at the local one but had to go to the main office for the appropriate paperwork.

She had discussed with me that her vehicle was pulled over by a couple of Policemen and they had questioned her, asking where she was coming from, her age, what movie she went to see, etc.

Although those questions were not appropriate questions to ask, but once they were done, they began dishing out tickets. It was a black movie they had already heard about and so many were in disagreement with it, and she felt she was treated unfairly. After the questioning and the tickets, her car was impounded. She had her younger brother in the vehicle with her and he had already seen so much from police officers and how they handled his father and his siblings. She had said how they kept shining the light on him, etc.

But never-the-less, when she called and asked if I could take her, I had already committed to without thinking about it. After I thought of what I just did, I said, oh man, because I was planning to rest today *(This rose was concerned).*

My other granddaughter had brought her to my apartment and we went from there. As we entered the place, I saw the many people sitting in there and I told her, that I will be waiting in my car. After waiting for more than two hours, I was getting hungry. I went inside to see how further along she was. She didn't know because she wasn't given a number, so she was unsure. I looked to the right side of me and saw a couple eating a sandwich and asked them where they got it. I left to go and as I was beginning to pull off, my granddaughter then came out and jumped in the car. So, the both of us rode to the burger place to get something to eat. Hoping that they never called her name. When we returned, she went back inside. After waiting over three hours, her name was finally called.

It was just to sign a paper to prove that she had insurance, etc. We then were on our way to the police department. We were told by an officer that the car wasn't there, it was at another location. But we had to go to the police department first then take the paper to get the car. This meant that I was gone all day. During all of this, my son had called.

He wanted to go to the hospital to see my niece. After returning with my granddaughter, I went home to rest. Then he called. I at first was planning to go with them, but my body was really tired. *(This rose is now weary).* So, when I picked them up, they came back to my apartment and ate. I then told them to go ahead and can use my car to go see my niece because I was too tired to even ride in the backseat.

Later on, I was wondering where they were, come to find out my sister had been dropped off and my son had taken my car home with him. I was upset at first because it seemed that neither had let me know what was going on and I felt someone should have called me. Maybe they thought I would be too tired to take them back home, I'm not sure. But it got me a little upset. I then went to bed. This is all to show just how much the enemy can use whom he likes to wear us down.

(This rose was in a fighting to win mode).

The following morning, my phone was ringing, and it was my son. He said that he had tried ringing the bell where I live and calling my phone, but I wouldn't answer. My phone was down on silent and I did not realize it. When I did picked up, he had called from my sister's phone to let me know that he was at her house. He later came to return my car. After getting the keys from him, I came back into my apartment.

He didn't come inside my apartment but had informed me of some things. I felt frustrated because of some incidents that had occurred. I had to later apologize. Later that day I received a text from my former supervisor. She asked had I thought about applying for my former boss's position. It was so strange because she and the female that took over after she left, had texted me at the same time about the same thing. It had crossed my mind because of what they had taken me through, but I didn't think any more about it.

I made a phone call or two to ask for prayers regarding the matter. They both advised me of the same thing. So, I revised my resume and I sent it to a couple of people to ask their opinions on it. One replied and answered me but the other has not, as of yet answered.

I then submitted my Resume to the director. Before the day was over, I received an email from her asking about me coming in for an interview. I didn't know how to feel. I somewhat got excited, but fear did set in because I told God; that's a big step for me to take. I know that God has something great in store for me. There was a vision that he showed me when I was working for the State of New Jersey, I saw myself going through these cherry pine double doors and I was sitting behind this cherry wood large desk. I knew that the challenge would be a great one.

But although fear sat in, I still know that God can deliver and sit me in places where I thought I would never sit.

That next day, I had forgotten about a training I had to attend on my job. This meant that I could not attend Bible study. So, I texted the Pastor and told him. I didn't hear from him, so I called him. He stated that he did get the message. I mentioned to him about the interview, and he said, "Start thanking God." He asked me if I'll be off on Sundays, and to make sure that I would be. I then later spoke with my former supervisor and mentioned Sunday's to her. She stated, that I will be on call 24/7. But if this is what God has for me, He will not allow anyone or anything to jeopardize the time I give to Him.

I later went to the training on the job. Some things happened at the training that seemed so unreal. But I told God, that if He wants me to have this position, He has to really deal with those employees that were being oppositional already. And if they were already, they will be the same ones that will be oppositional then. I told God that I am really going to need His help in this, because I have no idea how to handle such a large position. *(This rose felt a little withered).*

Chapter Ten

"Me, Being the Target"

It was that Friday that I had an interview. Prior to going on the interview, I made sure that I could come because we had a nor'easter storm a day or two before. But I did get the email stating that it was still on. I really wanted someone to go with me, but God did not allow that. Upon arriving, another female was coming out of the interview room. The secretary at the desk was nice and very mannerly to me. She asked if I wanted some water, and if I had to use the restroom.

At first the director came downstairs and then the other female that was interviewing. The questions they were asking seemed normal. I had to really think but was able to answer them accordingly. One of the other ladies asked about the title of one of my books. I, for one do not remember a lot of things, since my sister was murdered. (Her death traumatized me just that much) so I had to pull the book out, give the name and what the Three Rs represented.

After the interview, I shook hands with the both of them and thanked them. On my way home, I called my former supervisor and told her how it went. She said to ask if I was hired for the position, would interrupt my pastoring on Sundays.

When I called the director back, she said that it should not, but that I will be on call 24/7. To me, I left that in Gods' hands. In a way I wanted it, but in another sense, I did not because of the great responsibilities and how it might put a damper on what I am already doing for domestic violence.

When I went into work that next day, I had already sensed that there was talk about me, which I am accustomed to by now. But felt that it was already told to some that I had applied for the position. On my way home that Saturday night, I had to go by to pick up two of my grandchildren. I happened to go on the street where my friend lived. He was a friend of about 20 plus years. He and I would talk periodically. At times he would pick me up and take me for a ride just to get my mind off things. There were times we would just ride out of state just for the scenery. But he was only a friend.

It seemed strange that when I got to the light, a vehicle was coming the opposite direction, and they had the right of way to turn, but they hesitated. So, I waited. I sensed that my friend was in that vehicle. The tags were out of state tags. They always talk about that state. But the vehicle went right by the house. That was a dead give-a-way because he knows my vehicle so he would not let that vehicle stop at his place knowing that I was behind them. *(This rose was tested).*

It did not matter who he was with, because we are only friends and I was not going to stop or call him to ask who was in the vehicle? Where did you go? Etc. I had explained that to him before. Both of us talk to the opposite sex and our belief system is different. Friends are friends through the good, the bad and the indifferent. Now we laugh about it. We're just friends! Point blank! I kept going and went to pick them up.

I knew that earlier that day, as I went to a store at the mall. I parked my vehicle, and as I was walking by another vehicle, I heard the engine on. I did not pay attention to the vehicle until after I went by, and I sensed that it was his vehicle. I had looked partly around my shoulder and noticed that it was his. I wondered why he did not speak. I felt that maybe he had someone in his vehicle and did not want me to know; since he is a private individual. I frowned on the matter, thinking if I should turn around and speak or what. When he gets ready to talk, he knows how to contact me.

Until then, I will continue to do what God is leading me to do without unnecessary distractions.

Chapter Eleven

"My Struggles and Strengths"

It's going into Sunday morning. I had service and God really blessed. My sister and the both of my grandchildren were there along with their father and a friend of his. After service, I fed them and went to work. When I went into work, I felt that something wasn't right when I went inside of the building. I made up in my mind that I was going to start staying to myself and do as little talking as possible, not unless it was concerning my job and the clients. Of course, I was questioned as to why I was quiet. But when you sense the enemy at work, you do not play in his hands or give him ammunition to use against you.

It was that following week when we had a staff meeting, when I first went into the building, and I could tell that it was told to some about me applying for the position. Some stopped talking and came out of the room. During the meeting, there were a lot of questions asked and, in my observation, they were legit questions. But, I also saw some things that were not right. I had made up in my mind that God, if you want me to have this position, I would prefer that it be at a neutral place where I am not known. The reason for this is because I was already told how some of the employees there had sabotaged other employees that came through there and ran them out.

Not that they would run me out, it would be that they would make sure they would not cooperate with my orders or what I would ask them to do. At a different location, I know that I would get a fresh start. Knowing that it would not be up to the people whether I was qualified or not, but it would be up to God *(God is strengthening the fight in this rose).* Man does not have a say-so in the matter of who, where or when I should or should not have or be in a position. Well, I know that God has, is and will be good to me either way. What is for me is for me regardless of who like it. *(This rose is gaining confidence and the pedals are getting their strength back).*

When I went home that night, I saw that my grandchildren were still up. I told them that they had to go to bed because they had school the next morning.

After we woke up the next morning I took both of them to school, with the oldest being first, then the youngest. After dropping the youngest off, before I pulled off, I saw that she was still standing outside. I backed up to ask if she could go inside. She said no because the school doors were not open yet for them to go inside. So, we went to get breakfast. Then I dropped her back off. It was during that week that I wanted to just rest.

Later on, during the week a friend of mine called asking if I could take her to a friend's house.

Her friend was placed on hospice care and the Lord let her know that this was the day she had to go see her. When we went, the both of us was glad because my friend took it a little hard but thank God that I was there to pray for her and sense a peace come over her. We then left and went to get a bite to eat. While sitting in the parking lot, another one of her friends came and she and her baby went with her. It was okay with me because I knew that I was in her life for a season. That season ended not too, long after that.

Later, during the end of the week, I spoke to my son. He told me that he had contemplated suicide. But he had a dream that night about my sister that was murdered. The dream was, he went to where she was. He said that, the both of them hugged, and she told him how she was glad to see him. She told him to tell me hello and how she missed the family. He also said that she had on a pretty emerald green gown and she was so pretty. She also told him that he is going to be alright. I reminded him of how the enemy tried to pull him into suicidal states before when his friend was killed. And I also told him that if he had of committed suicide, that his kids would be left behind to suffer. I reminded him how close his younger children are to him and to leave them like that, he would not know what state of mind he would leave them in. He said, "WOW, I didn't think about that."

I know that the enemy did not want me to remind him of it either. Satan just wants his soul, but I told him that God has great things in store for him and he cannot leave here until God does through him what He wants to do. It gave him something to think about. I realize how much he loves his children, and although his two younger children were not in his care at the time, I also realize exactly how much he misses them. *(This rose got emotional allowing the dew from the weather to leak a couple drops).*

Chapter Twelve

"God Kept Death Away"

It was later into this year that I was dealing with a lot of pain in my neck and right arm. At times I would be holding something in my right hand, but my hand would give out and I would drop whatever I was holding. I went to see my primary doctor and she referred me to a neurologist. When I went to the doctor she referred, he recommended that I need to have two surgeries. One to the front of my neck and other to the back. I really did not want to hear that, but he showed me the test taken and it showed where 3 to 4 of the discs in my neck area had degenerated. That the type of operation would be a Neck Infusion Surgery.

I kept putting it off because I wanted to continue working. But after while it got to the point where I could no longer work. I could not grab nor pickup things without dropping them and I was in so much pain. Before having the surgery, I went to Philadelphia to get a second opinion. The doctor I saw told me that the front of my neck surgery I needed, but not to get the second one done, not unless I really needed it. But for right now, I did not need it. So, when I went to inform my neurological doctor, he agreed to wait for the second surgery, but kept insisting that I should have it done.

Nevertheless, I had to take a leave of absence from my job by going on sick leave. During the time the doctor wanted to schedule the surgery, I asked him to hold off because of the domestic violence event that I already had scheduled.

That following Monday, October 8, 2018, I went into the hospital that morning to have the scheduled surgery done. My daughter had taken off to take me and stay there until after my surgery. My oldest son had gone with her; although he was not up to it, but he did it to support me. It was not until after the surgery and I had recovered, that my daughter explained to me what had happened. She said, "mom, they brought you into the Recovery room around 1:00pm but you didn't come through recovery until after 8:00pm. Then they had to give you Narcan to bring you through. But after you woke up, the first thing you asked for was oxtails." I'm like, "WHAT??? I remember coming through and seeing her falling on my bed laughing, but I, at the time did not know why. My son also said to me, "Mom, they lost you on that table." He said, "They had you in the Intensive Care Unit (ICU). They would not have had you in there unless they had lost you and they would not have had all of those tubes in you if they had not of lost you." I told both my daughter and son what I had experienced while on the table. I told them that while I was on the operation table that three things I experienced.

The first thing was, I saw the word "die." I then saw the second which was the word "died". The third thing was, I remembered telling God that, "I cannot leave here yet because my work here isn't done." Those were the only things I remembered while I was out *(This rose had died but God revived her).*

Upon my discharge, which was on the third day, I could not lift my neck at all without support. My daughter helped me for a few days, then she asked my next door neighbor to help me. There were also times when my grandson came and stayed a few nights. Although I was well taken care of, there were some that could have helped but did not. I remember, about a few months or so afterwards going to a church service for my niece who was in a nursing home. Her church had given her an appreciation service and I went to support her. When I went, I had to wear a neck brace. I remember going into the church and saw on a couple faces a smirk. At that time, I did not care because God had worked a miracle in me, and I made up in my mind that I did not care what others thought. Yet, there were many there who were very compassionate. I thank God how He brought me through what He did. My doctor still talks about having the other surgery. But they lost me on the table the 1st time and there was no way I was giving them the opportunity to lose me a second time.

Chapter Thirteen

"Emotional Drops"

It was after a lot of my healing process took place, when there were many days I would go to my oldest son's house and talk to him about his children and about his father whom he lost. He constantly thinks about his father, because the both of them were very close. And before his father died, he would go to his house to help his stepmother out with him. Prior to his father dying, they would do things together such as go fishing, ball games and just hang out together. There were also times when they went to church together. Although his father and I did not remain in the marriage, (we divorced in June 3,1985 the day of his birthday) I remember once the judge granted me the divorce, a joy came up in my spirit.

I was still in love with my husband, but that wasn't who God wanted me to continue to be with and didn't want me to go through anymore with him. We had three children together and a fourth, whereas, I had a miscarriage. When I miscarried, God spoke to me, letting me know that it was a boy. For whatever reason, God would not allow me to have children out of wedlock. It was not until his later years that he and I were able to come together to settle the differences that we had. It was during the time I was holding a Bible Study that turned into a church service he attended.

He was my main supporter, by keep calling out, "Amen," and agreeing to what I was preaching on. After the service that night, he came up to me and the both of us had a discussion, and he apologized. From that day on, we began getting along and became the best of friends.

I was telling my son that every time I would see his father in the store or somewhere in the public or at his house, that he would always kiss me on the cheek. I said, "Boy he had some sloppy kisses!" But my son and I would always laugh about it. But reminiscing now about my past, my ex-husband was a good-hearted person. It wasn't until his later years that he understood who I really was. And although he would thank me for raising our children; my son would say how he would brag on the good job I did of raising them. But he didn't leave himself out of it. He said, "Mom, that would make me mad because you had to raise us all alone, exception for the few years I was with him." Well, if that made him happy by saying that, Oh well! To me, bygones will be bygones, let him have that. *(The pedals on this rose stood up).*

I later began seeing how my son was going down-hill, concerning his health, along with dress code and his living conditions. It had gotten to the point where he didn't have heat nor electricity.

And what made me upset about that was, of all of the people going and coming in and out of his house, no one would give him a dime to help out with a bill nor food. He would tell me, "Mom they hate to see you coming". This was because I would go into his home to talk to all who were there about what they were taking him through; and to discuss what their lifestyles were like. Asking some, if they were in college, looking for employment, or just hanging around doing nothing. I explained to them that I wasn't there to judge, but to see them doing things that wasn't right and the intelligence they had, they could be doing much better. Many took heed to what I was saying and agreed with me. I was also explaining to them about how they were doing their business outside, during broad daylight and the cops were watching them.

At one point, when the police had to come to his house, I told the police that I told the guys there that they were watching them. The police officer just looked at me. I told them that I was not trying to avoid them from doing their job, but if I can help get some of the guys off the streets that that would make their jobs much easier. The ones I told that too, they understood my presence of being there (in no ways were I trying to block or hinder what they had or planned to do). But my method of getting them off the streets were encouraging them to get back in school, gain employment or a trade of some type.

And, if they needed help in doing so, I would help them or direct them where to go or to the right person. *(This rose realized that everyone isn't an enemy).*

It got to the point where I didn't care if they hated to see me coming because he would not, for some reason, defend himself. It was like he was just giving up on life. I really believed that this was because of the death of so many people he lost in his life, which included his five children's mother, his father, all four grandparents, his brother-in-law, some of his friends and many people that he knew.

There were times when I went to his house and instead of some of them leaving, the Lord had me to Minister to them or they would want prayer. But neither time did I look down on either of them. There were maybe 2 or 3 friends he had that I saw was really trying to help him, but even with that they were limited. It was getting cold and the temperatures were dropping. I told him that he cannot stay with me, but he can come over so that I can help him take better care of himself. Due to my own living arrangements he could not stay in the apartment building I was living in. It got to the point where I went to talk to the manager about him being there. I explained his condition to her, and she told him what he needed to do.

I still let him come at times to make sure he was eating, bathing and keep his doctor appointments. Me and his oldest daughter would take turns helping him out. Also, this was a way that he would be in church on Sundays.

I remember when the Thanksgiving holiday came that he didn't want to have anything to do with family. *(This rose was bearing pain of her son).* But he got through that. Christmas came and his kids wanted him to come to my daughter's house for the holiday. I encouraged him to come and he was so thankful that he did. While there for the Christmas holiday, my granddaughter took a picture with all three of my children in the same picture. They laughed and talked, and it was a day to remember. It made me feel good to be able to always have my children together in one room, because they all had busy schedules.

The end of December, during his youngest son's birthday, I was in a store and while going up to the counter, I ran into my daughter. She and I left out together and stood outside and had a conversation about different things. She then informed me that my grandson wanted me to bake him a # 17 cake and he wanted Ambrosia salad. I was surprised because I didn't think he liked it. But he did. And that was a joy to me, to be able to do the things that make them smile.

He was turning 17 years old, and my daughter at first she wanted to take him out to dinner and had invited me and my son. But since I told her that the doctor wanted my son to be hospitalized, his son decided to wait for the dinner. (*This rose became emotional with dew drops throughout these months).*

I remember the day of his birthday and his son called me asking, "Grandma, is my dad still there?" I told him yes. He asked, "Is it okay If we come there to eat my birthday cake and ice cream?" I told him yes! I was so happy he wanted his dad to be a part of his birthday celebration. Those moments meant so much to all of us. But one thing my grandson did, was bring over peanut butter ice cream! I was like, "WHAT???? I told him that I only like peanut butter and jelly together. But since we are starting a new year, I will get accustomed to starting new things." Everyone laughed at me. After tasting it, it wasn't so bad after all.

I was able to take a picture of my son, my daughter and grandson together. That made me feel really grateful. Even as the months progressed, at times he would see his children and at times he would just cry because he missed them. But I would always try to encourage him of the things he needed to do. Sometimes he would get upset with me and there were times we would just sit back, laugh and talk about things in general.

I love all three of my children and know that they love me. Sometimes as a parent, our children don't always understand certain things or ways they had to go, but, neither do we as parents. It's always a touch and go, a hands on and a stern speech that parents have to give their children. But there were so many times that I would run into people in the community, that they would always tell me how my children are so respectful and would commend me for doing a great job in raising them.

Sometimes I would cry, because having to raise them alone wasn't always easy. I had to take the bitter with the sweet at times. Sometimes it was more bitter than sweet because I would not compromise with my children and would not let go of being a firm parent. There were times we cried, prayed and just hugged each other. There were many times my children would thank me for doing a great job in raising them and remind me of things I did or told them that helped them in today's world. They would tell me about the strength I held as a black woman and how I would go to bat for them. But they would never see the pain I went through behind parenting, nor did they see me cry.

They saw my strength, the courage, my battles, my hurt, my fears, my persecutors, my faults and my maintaining my milestones of overcoming.

I give all the Glory and Honor to God. Because every day I would pray about my children and cry out to God on their behalf. One thing I realized was, God and my children were my world…Nobody knew that! And when grandchildren and great-grands came, I protected them as well, the best that I knew how. But I did cover them in prayer and in love. *(This rose went through a milestone of strength—BUT GOD)!*

As the months progressed, I saw even more of a deterring in my son. And as a parent, I see the pain that he carried, also, the pain in my heart of wanting to help, but could not. My other children would tell me to stop worrying about him because I would run the risk of becoming sick with worry. But I guess as a parent who raised her children, there was always a mother hen's mentality to always want to protect. But I had to learn to do just that; to stop worrying and give him to God.

As the months flew by, his health was getting worse; where he did not want to go to the doctor, hospital or whatever help he needed. *(This rose needs strength).*

Going back a few months, during the early part of the month of August, I received a call from my sister. She had informed me that her son was killed in an auto accident the night before. She had received a call early that morning. I was devastated!

He was my second oldest nephew. I called my daughter and my sons to inform them. I think everyone was so numb. He was the life of almost every event he attended. He always laughed. Every time you would see him; he was laughing or smiling. Always cracking jokes. But the family had gotten into a numb state trying to accept the fact that he had passed. When I saw his uncles, my sisters, etc., no one could believe what had happened. Someone had sent me a copy of the video of the scene. I had so many questions regarding what had occurred, as well as so many others. It was so hard that week. My sister had asked if I could say something at the funeral. I thought about it and told her that I'd rather not I didn't think that I could handle it. *("Yes, even as a pastor, certain things are devastated and hard to adjust to.")*

Now prior to the days of the funeral, I had taken my brother to Camden to see a friend of his who was hospitalized in ICU. Upon returning to my sister's house, I was standing at the counter in the kitchen. Her niece had asked me what my title was? I told her pastor, and asked why? She said so I will have your name right on the obituary. I looked at my sister and she said, "Oh, I want you to say something at his funeral because you're a Minister." I did not say no, I said okay. I really did not know what to say because, all of a sudden, my mind went blank.

Although I've known him all of his life, everything just went blank from my mind. There was a lot I could have said, but I wasn't sure. I began calling different ones about finding out things about him because I wanted to write a poem. I tried writing two or three poems but couldn't get it together. I did end up writing a poem, but writing what God gave me, verses what other people wanted me to write. *(This rose was weathering the storm).*

Chapter Fourteen

"A New Beginning"

Starting back up in 2020;

We started the New Years by having service in the dining hall. It was only about 4 or 5 of us, but we had a nice time. Starting the morning, I felt a little angry because my son wanted his friend of over 20 years to stay the night since it was already going into the am hour. I allowed it, but became angry because when they were leaving service, they escorted my sister outside. I came upstairs to my apartment.

As I was getting onto the elevator, my phone rang. It was a male friend calling to wish me a Happy New Year. I wished him the same. But getting back to my son, it took them the longest to come back upstairs, to the point where I automatically felt they started to return to my son's house or go places they should not have gone. *(This rose is feeling a lot of tension).*

When they finally came upstairs, my son knew that I was furious. He tried to explain that when he was downstairs in the bathroom that he fell asleep on the toilet (*something he had been doing a lot of lately)*. But God had to calm me down. Just starting the New Year off, I did not want to start it off this way. But, to God be the Glory. He knows all things.

I just have to let go and let God be God when it comes to my children. This year I had made up in my mind that I just had to feel human and not try to be strong for everybody other than myself. *(This rose was nourished back to health).*

Well, after my son and his male friend had stayed the night, I took the both of them home the next day. I wasn't angry, but I did have to explain to them that as a single woman, and as a Pastor, I needed them to understand that I cannot leave my door unlocked waiting for them to come in. And when they do this, it breaks my rest and it is unsafe. I really needed them to hear this, especially my son. They understood and the both of them apologized.

It seemed like during the beginning of this year, that I was feeling alone so much. I felt that no one was there for me. Although I was introduced to a male friend, it was still hard for me. I had told God many days that I felt so lonely and alone. I asked, "GOD, WHERE ARE YOU? Why am I feeling so alone? What season of my life that I am in now?

It then came to me that during this time in my life that I had to be very careful not to get out of the will of God. I had to come to the knowledge that when we are feeling alone and deal with the opposite sex, the enemy would try to throw you a curve ball into your life to distract you and get us off course.

But one thing that God did do (not saying that He didn't do many), was to keep my mind stayed on Him. To constantly pray. I thank God that I did because Satan had some traps set up for me. God reminded me that it is okay to feel lonely, but I am never alone. He reminded me that He will never leave me nor forsake me, even during my lonely and feeling alone days. *(The struggling Rose).*

Sometimes, this would be my prayer:

"God, right now I feel alone. There are times I just wanted to be held. No hanky panky, but just someone (the opposite sex) just to hold me. I do get tired of being by myself and I do get tired of walking this walk by myself. I know that you are there, but there are those times that I wish you could come down and just sit and talk to me. I know that you do talk to me, minister to me and encourage me, but there are those moments when I just need your presence right now. I need you just to hold me and let me know that everything is going to be alright.

To hear you say that I hear your prayer, that I hear you crying and that you are there just to comfort me, like a mother would do for her child that's afraid of the dark, or like a father, to give his daughter that reassurance. But Father, I still thank you because what I am going through right now, it is only for a season. I know that my breakthrough is somewhere up the road.

I know that you will see me through all of this, in Jesus Name, Amen."*(This rose was taught how to pray).* During this time, many tears are flowing down my cheek.

There were times also I felt that no one really wanted to be bothered with me. This included my children and anyone of the nature. I needed and wanted someone to love me through my pain. Love me through my hurt; not try to hold me accountable for my hurt but love me through it. Can anyone just accept me for me? Can anyone just love on me just because of me without having a reason? I've heard of so many testimonies of how God allowed individuals to come into a person's life and accept them for being who they are. Is that such a hard thing for me? Just for being me?

It was during this time I was feeling angry towards different individuals because of how they handled me. Then on the other hand, I had to repent just as I at first felt the anger. I had to come to the reality that God doesn't always allow certain people to be there for you all of the time, because He wants all of the glory. The thought came to me that if He allowed certain people to be there for me like I wanted and expected them too, that they would get the credit and God said that He will not share His glory with no one.

So I had to accept the fact this was exactly the reason I had to endure certain things and that certain people could not put their hands in anything or in any way God choses to bless me. Yes, there were many lonely days, but I had to walk those days out by trusting God in the process. Sometimes, I get weak and struggle too! *(The rose that's standing alone).*

I would also run into people who would tell me how strong I was. *(Sometime when a person is going through, you don't want to hear how strong you are.)* If only they knew that I was hurting and just as human as they were. And there were times I had to actually tell them that. I would also tell them that the smile they see on me and the laughter they would see would only be temporarily because I hurt, cry, and have pain just like them.

Just because I am a Pastor doesn't mean that all of my days are like roses. *(This rose has tackled many trials)* I had to endure much pain, and still deal with a lot of pain, but I had to also not wear my pain on my sleeves, like I use too.

During the same week, I had a doctor appointment which went well except my pressure was high. My doctor ordered testing and more testing and more testing. After returning back home, I decided to look at my diet and how I was eating. It seemed that I was eating everything I felt that I could eat.

I had to realize that I am not getting younger, and now I have to really reconsider my diet. On my way home I spoke to my friend for a brief period of time. Then I decided to stay in for the remaining of the evening.

January, 2020--I am now going into another day of the year. Today I pray is a new beginning for my happiness. I had to meet a friend of mine to go over paperwork for something. She is expected here by 9:30. However, she did go over the paper as well as contacted the main office regarding my status and the things I had to do to come back into the business. The both of us were informed that I did not have to start from the beginning but all I needed to do was take the exam. Once I passed the exam, I can start where I left off from as Senior Claims Rep. Then if interested I can go to Regional Manager.

I am interested in starting again, but it's a lot I had to think about. It was also during the day that I got a couple calls from my male friend but I did not answer. I had a lot to deal with and a lot to think about. I know that what I want is to remain saved and stay with God. I did not want to in any way get involved with anyone at this point, especially if a third party was involved. Later that night I got a call from a male who I use to work with and the fact that he had been trying to get with me.

But every time he tried; he would always let me down; so, I refused to answer the phone. It was during the same day that I read an article of a murder-suicide. It was in the area where he lived. I thought that maybe he was calling about that, so I tried to contact him back. He never answered and I never tried again.

I had received a phone call from my male friend. He just called to say good morning. The phone woke me up. He stated that he would call me back later but during the day I had a very hard time with my phone, thinking that it had a virus. I took it to the phone store. After checking it out, they found out that I still had the warranty on it and could get a new phone, but the same type of phone, in which I did have them to order it.

After leaving the store, I went to another store in the same area. While there, I ran into my daughter, and she I had held a conversation. Upon leaving my daughter, I went back to my apartment and I called my male friend back.

I told him that I wanted us to start over again fresh. Our friendship originally started off with us being a help to each other spiritually, but it took a different turn of calling every day and it began to get too emotional and I began having feelings. So, I informed him that we have to take it back from the beginning, which was Spiritual.

But I do not want my name tarnished neither his. He agreed! He was informed as well as him informing me that if God decided that we get together, it would be up the road, if it was God's will. In the meanwhile, we will be focusing on going forward in God. But did agree that if either needed prayer, needed to talk or once in a while, we would call each other and be there for each other in that way. He stated how he respected me for that decision. He also let me know that if I needed him for anything, he would be there for me, and would help me out in whatever way I needed him.

After our conversation I felt relieved. I knew that Satan really wanted it to go another way, but I thank God that He prepared me and showed me several visions of how the enemy tried to plant a trap for me concerning this person. I didn't share this with him about all of what God had showed me; neither did I feel led too.

After returning home, I then went inside and rested for a while. My son then came in and asked if he could have company for an hour. I told him at first no because I was tired and didn't want any company. I then received a text from one of my members, where I had to go and pickup something from her. So, then I told my son that he could have company because I had to leave.

Upon my returning, both he and his friend were there. They were watching football. After a while, they left to go outside and smoke, then go downstairs to watch football in the dining area. Later, my son's friend came up first stating that two women downstairs came into the dining area where they were. My son had left to go into the bathroom, but his friend said that the ladies said that they weren't supposed to be in the dining area without me being there. I told him, that it was the truth. That you are my company and I am responsible for your actions while you are in this building. When my son came in, it was told what had occurred and he became angry. I told him not to because they were right this time.

Sunday came and my son got up and was getting ready for church. Church service was good. I had a chance to explain to those that were there how I felt. How they didn't really respect me as their leader; meaning that some of them still do what they want and weren't trying to do right. They disregarded my concerns; yet, they tell me that they want me to continue being their Pastor and leader. Not to put guilt on them but I cannot allow them to burn me out. They agreed and also agreed to step up.

After service, I stayed home and was laying down on the couch. Both my son and his friend stayed there. Then the Lord spoke with me about going to another service, which was a prayer service.

As I was leaving, I informed my son to make sure my door was locked when it was time to go with his daughter. As I was driving, my phone rang. It was my male friend. He asked had I planned to stay in or go to another service. I was beginning to get curious because he began asking me the same questions. I told him I wasn't sure yet. I didn't want him to know my every move. While there, God really blessed; He used me to Minister to the Pastor and his wife. I then left afterwards and went home. I stayed in the rest of the evening.

Chapter Fifteen

"Fighting Feelings"

It was Monday morning and I had an early doctor's appointment to get a TB test and bloodwork done. I was hired part time on a new job. Afterwards I went to renew my registration. Upon returning home, I stopped by the office where I lived. The manager called me inside and told me that the two women had a problem with my son and his friend watching television without me being there with them. She also told some other things and gave me information about the women. It was decided that my son could no longer be at my apartment. I did not want to say anything to him at first but thought about it. I had to go back out and get water and other items. I returned back and thought about what my neighbor had said at the church service where I had visited. I called her, asking if I could come talk with her. She said yes.

I asked her about what she had said. We had discussed the situation and I left it alone. We were able to get some things straightened out, I thought; along with her saying things towards me. Some things God had already dealt with me about, which I knew wasn't right, but I would not say or do anything to hurt her or anyone.

My son called me later to see how I was doing. At first, I could hardly hear him because of his grandchildren. But I had to end up telling him what the manager had said and the things that had been happening here, that he could no longer spend time here, but he had to leave. I told him he had three weeks to be here. He was a little upset at first and stated. "I knew something like this was going to happen. People are going to reap what they sow." I told him that it was not that, it is the fact that you have to take on your own responsibility. You have to be the one that have to pull yourself up and do what's right. I know that people are going to be people, but it is not their responsibility to make things right for other people.

I explained to him that God had already showed him who the people were in his life. He is worried about family. I told him that it is not family's responsibility it is his. God showed him that family is not what they use to be. He was a little hurt, but understood, to a degree. But I know that he will be okay. *(This rose is feeling the pressure).*

I explained to him that he has to do what is right and get his daughter to help him with certain things. I love my son, but he has to realize that he can't depend on people to do for him, he is an adult.

I saw something that made me upset with him. It was a few days ago when he told me how sick he was. But he made a move that shocked me. I won't go into detail about what he did in order to respect his privacy. But I knew that something different had to take place, other than what I saw. What he did bothered me greatly, and I took it personally. I am trying to help him, and he let other people interfere with his health. Even his doctor kept calling me to make sure he is okay and how he is trying to get him into a hospital so he can get the proper care. But he kept refusing. My thing is that if you are not trying to help yourself, how can you expect others to help you?

It is a new day and today was one of those days I decided to stay inside all day. I was tired from taking the medication the doctor had prescribed a few days ago for diabetes and high blood pressure. I had made up in my mind that I was going to eat better. I made up my mind that I will be eating less carbs and starches. I have decided to take better care of my health. While at home, my other son came by wanting me to help him with a project. He then left. I tried but did not want to put the wrong information into the computer. I kept trying but could not get the right things to work; but kept in contact with him letting him know about what was happening.

I later got a call from my male friend. He said that he really wanted to call me because he was going through; but promised me that he would not call me every day. I explained to him that if it was for prayer, that was a different story. I will help and pray for anyone who needs prayer. This has been an exceedingly difficult situation. I have been praying about this from day one and I know that I have to take my time with him. I cannot rush into anything, and most of all I have to be prayerful because the adversary will try to get me in a situation to make it seem like it's one thing, but it's something else. I have been down that road, and I cannot afford to go down that same road again, spiritually or in the natural.

January 8, 2020 @ 3:11am

Today is my nephew's birthday who is incarcerated. He did ended up calling me and I was able to wish him a happy birthday. Every time I speak with him, such a joy comes over the both of us. Because when I would see him, he always had this laugh and smile that would make anyone smile. He always looked up to me as his mother ever since I began raising him after she was murdered. It always felt that he fit right into our family. Not as a nephew but as another son and my children took to him as one of their siblings.

He also wanted me to try to find out information on who were his doctors, psychiatrists, schools he attended, the babysitters and other physicians who he had seen while he was in my care. I promised him that I would find out that information because his public defender needed it.

Later, my male friend also called me just to say hello. Although we promised not to be on the phone every day, he would always find a way to call me and to make me laugh. One of the things I found out about him was, that the hurt and pain I had been experiencing from my past, God was using him to help me through the healing process. There would be things that he would say would always keep me thinking and, matter-of-fact, he would be on point. I don't know what God's plan was for the both of us, but I do know one thing for certain, and that is that I knew how to laugh again without feeling guilty. He would always say that he promised me to never hurt me but would be there for whatever reason I would need him. I told him how I appreciated that!

Still during the early part of this year, I had returned back to the doctor for the second and third time after my surgery, I told him that fluid was in my upper back. He checked and agreed. He said, "Yes, there is some fluid there, but wait until the main doctor who did the surgery check it out."

I asked him, "what will or could he do about it." He said, "he will probably take a needle and withdraw it or may have to give me another minor surgery." I told him, "you are not cutting on me again. You lost me the first time on the table, why would you want to give me another surgery after that." He really could not answer.

It was not too long after that where I had to go to my primary doctor. During this time, I was somewhat wheezing. I told her about the fluid, and she checked my chest and back with her stethoscope. She held it on my back longer than usual. When she stopped and said, "You're alright!" I knew that she was not telling me the truth because a stethoscope can detect things the normal hearing cannot. At that point I stopped trusting her.

It was during this week that I had begun experiencing a lot of coughing and blowing my nose. It was not so much of coughing that bothered me, but what bothered me was the mucus. When I would lay down, I had to get up and blow my nose; after blowing my nose, thick greenish mucus would come out. This was going on so much to the point that I told my son. When he saw it, he said, "mom, that's pneumonia". I could not do nothing but thank and praise God. It could have been a lot worse or remain in my lungs, but God! Never had pneumonia, so I did not know what the fluids looked like.

Thank God, He allowed it to come through my nose. *(This rose is so thankful).*

This is another day that God allowed me to arise. During this day, I was called in to do my paperwork for my new job. Upon completing my paperwork and getting another tour of the facility, I was asked if I could start my orientation the following day. I was pleased and said yes! I was excited about the job. I did not share my excitement with too many people because I knew that some would not be happy for me. The idea of knowing that I was able to obtain an income to help out with my excess bills seemed to have been a problem for some people.

Later that day I told my male friend my excitement and he was as excited for me. It was later that day that my son came over so I could help him complete the process for his paperwork. He later text me to look up a definition for him. I did and text it to him. He was getting ready to begin his own business. I was SO happy for him. I had been telling him that he was supposed to have this business years ago. He said, "I know." But nevertheless, he has it now, and I thank God for that.

Early the next morning, my male friend called me just to say hello and gave me his blessings. I later went into work; whereas, I was dealing with children from ages 2 to 5 years old.

For it being my first day, it took a toll on me and I was so exhausted by the time I got home. I had to figure out how to work the job, instead of letting the job work me. After returning home from work, my other son needed a phone for his business, so I went to the store with him to help him out. It was still during this time that my eldest son was still there at my house. He later cooked for me to make sure that I had a hot meal when I arrived. I thanked him for that, but I was too exhausted to talk.

After waking up the next day, I went into work that morning and, again, when I came home, I was exhausted. But for some reason, the phone company had put my name on my son's phone instead of his business name. My son had text me and I in return called the phone company and they corrected the error. But the same problem still existed. I ended up going down to the phone store and had them to correct it there, in which they did. The same problem occurred again. This time I had to call the company to make sure they were putting the right information in correctly. They did and he was alright afterward. He had asked about his brother, showing concern. He stated how he's on his mind but there was only so much he could do. He also stated how he had to be careful when and how he would go see him. Although my oldest son was at my house, my youngest son did come by periodically to visit him.

He would tell me how it bothered him to see him like that. My daughter was the same way. It bothered her to see her oldest brother looking like that.

It was during this time that my daughter was handling her business and I was able to be there for her. It was between the January and March months of 2020 that much had been happening. I was concerned a lot about my children and grandchildren. It was difficult starting a new job, trying to adjust myself and adjust my time. The church was moving along okay. Not a lot of members, but the ones there seems to be getting what they needed. I had asked the congregation questions about if they were learning from my Preaching? They said yes! I explained to them that I am there for them, but they acted like they didn't appreciate me. I had to pick up people for church, sometimes making more than one trip for pickup and drop-off. I had to do praise and worship, preach, pray for the individuals then return them home. It was a lot and it was beginning to take a toll on me.

It was during this time the attendance had increased, but I was tired, wanted to give up and, being honest, frustrated. I know that many may have said that I shouldn't be feeling that way. But let the truth be told? We as leaders need breaks and need to slow down so that the Lord can replenish us.

We have some members who still want to play pitty-pat with danger. They haven't had enough of the world to stop doing what they're doing, and not enough of God to want to stop. But be reminded that we are living in the last days where there are actual wars and rumors of wars and I was being fought with both. *(This rose fighting in the spirit).*

Chapter Sixteen

"God's Struggling Servants"

I am finding out that some of those wars are right in the house of God. The fighting, gossiping, hurting those who want to come in and won't because of how the congregation behaviors are. I remember back in the day, if we did then, what the church is doing now, the mothers of the church would easily rebuke us. Where are the mothers of the church today? They would sit us down and we would have to get on our knees and tarry. We would have to call on Jesus until we got delivered.

Today, a person can go to the Altar say a quick prayer and now their saved. But what are they saved from if they didn't mean it from the beginning? Did some go to the Altar just to look good, or to impress the pastor or to impress a family member? Because once they returned back home, they began doing the same things they did before they went to the Altar. All of this is helping me to stay saved. Not because of wanting to be seen, but to be an example of what Christianity is really about. I pray that God continue to keep me on a daily basis and not allow anyone to pluck me out of his hands.

When I desire to do evil *(which sometimes I have been fought with that)*, that God will turn my heart back to doing what it is that He is requiring me to do. When I become upset about a situation *(I have thought those thoughts),* that He reminds me to have the thoughts of Himself. But God! I know that He loves me so much that He guides me in the directions He has for me to go; and teaches me what He wants me to know. And since I started working, He Is working a new work in me. A work of much needed patience and understanding of younger children. *(boy, this rose is struggling!).*

My new job at first was a challenge, but I'm loving what I do. Dealing with infants, toddlers and up to pre-school ages would actually tire me out. But for some odd reason, it was a good tiring experience. I enjoyed making the children laugh and to see a smile when they have a hard time separating from their parents was something quite rewarding. There are excellent teachers that I work with. I sit and observe them, and I learn from them. Their patience and their teaching methods are tremendous. I have a very understandable and good supervisor; and all of this makes my job worth going to work for every day, worth the while. *(This rose is learning to be more tolerant).*

While on my job, I am learning the right routines of my job performance. My male friend always calls me to let me know how much I am appreciated. Sometimes it's hard to accept compliments when you've been wounded time and time again. It's hard to believe if one is really being honest with you; especially when you've been put down for so long. But only God knows. One thing he has helped me with and that is the pain of my past, it's no longer as painful.

We're now into the month of March and was told we're off Friday and Monday. We were told Monday that we were off until further notice due to the Coronavirus and how it was spreading throughout this country. Still in the month of March that for the next three days that I would not be making contact with my friend. The Lord had me on a type of fast that only He could have put me on, and it was through Him. It was a challenge, but it was necessary. He got me back into praying and reading His Word the way I needed to. I truly thank God for this time.

It is now Sunday morning and I had already contacted most of the church on yesterday to discuss having a phone conference call. Since no one was to be able to meet in groups, I thought it was a good idea to introduce the conference call as another option.

It was during the 11:00am hour that I was able to make the Conference Church Service Call. My oldest son's friend was able to go to my son's house and had many of them there listen at the church service from his phone. After the phone conference call, I was able to take my son a hot Sunday meal, which contained baked turkey wings, asparagus, candied yams and potato salad. While there he was standing by the refrigerator with his cane. He kept almost falling where at one point, he dropped his cane and I had to pick it up. A few people were there and one of the men was telling me how he was helping my son, etc. And I thanked him for being there for him. After making sure my son had gotten his meal, I kissed him and left.

After returning back home, one of my sisters texted me to let me know that my sister, who had never had a Facebook page, finally got on Facebook to put her message online. I was excited for her. And I as I usually do, I called one of my son's friends to see if he had a chance to talk to him. He said no but he will be going to see him tomorrow. I thanked him and realized the many hats that we may have to wear as parents, Pastors, siblings etc.

Later during this week, I reached out to my male friend. I hadn't talked with him for 3 days and he did not understand why.

I explained to him that it was the Lord's doing. He really wanted me to talk about it, but I could not. There will be times that the Lord will lead you away from a person or persons, and no explanation will be needed.

I had to call my bank about a transaction made and while on the phone with the female, she and I had a long talk. She was very professional and very understanding, along with the different transactions she had to put in for me that took quite a while. But I thank God for the conversation. The conversation really benefited the both of us.

I later received a personal text from my male friend and he called back to see if I had received it. I was shocked because he said that was his first time texting. He had explained before that he does not text. But I told him that he did a good job. Later during the day, a female friend of mine had called and later came over and had prayer with me. The Lord really used her to encourage me. *(This rose needs encouraging too!)*

Today, was a good day. First, my male friend called me. I had him laughing because of things he deals with and how he deals with them. There were points I brought to his attention that had him laughing. Laughter is such good medicine and anytime I can share a laugh is always a great day.

Later in the morning, I received a call from one of the men that my son does work for. He is an elderly 84 yr. old man. When he called, he said that I was on his mind. He said that he first asked my son if I would mind him calling me. My son told him that he didn't mind at all. He stated that he also asked God if he should call me. He said that God never gave him an answer, but God did tell him some about who I was. A couple days after the fact, he came by to bring my son to pick up his phone. The man had me laughing, but I also told my son that he is a fresh man. He was talking a lot of nonsense that day. But today when he called, he called with sense.

The conversation was a good, but he asked if I dated. I told him yes. So, of course, he asked if he could take me out to dinner one day. I told him, yes. As long as he stayed in his place. He said that he felt that I liked him. WRONG! I told him, that I am a people person and I get along with anybody. That does not mean that I like a person because I hold a decent conversation with them. He then went on to say that I am too nice and easy; and people take advantage of me. I did explain that I am too nice at times, but that does not mean that I am too easy. People just do not know who I am. Being nice, does not mean that I am easy. When they think that I am, things change up fast because they find out that being easy can easily get mistaken for being too nice.

We were on the phone for a little over an hour, holding a decent conversation. After hanging up, which he did not want to hang up because he said that he just needed a friend to talk with. As single Women, we must be careful of who we allow in our space. Some may get the wrong intentions, and it's a good practice to be honest in the very beginning, in which I was.

Later that day, I held a Conference Call for Bible Study that went well. My son then called and

I told him that his friend called me to talk. He said okay, and he told him that he was going to give men a call. I wanted to assure my son that I didn't mind as long as he kept things in the proper perspective and holds a decent conversation. Later, my male friend called to say goodnight. *(This rose is keeping it together).*

Chapter Seventeen

"Getting to Know Who We Are"

I woke up this morning, prayed and read my Bible. Made my bed then went into the living room to watch television. I received a call from my male friend. We laughed and carried on as usual. After getting off the phone, I went for a walk around the building I live in. After returning, he called back, asking if I went for a walk. He stated he went for a long walk himself. I then went on another walk; I walked to my sister's house, then to my son's to check on him, to the store and then returned back home. I then called my male friend back after I returned, but he seemed to want to get off the phone in a hurry, stating he had to prepare his dinner. He seemed a little deterred because I called. I accepted that and moved on with my day.

Later I received a call from a female pastor, stating that she had to go to Walmart. She asked if I wanted to ride with her. I told her yes, and upon her arrival, she called and I went downstairs. Upon us going to Walmart, she had to make a stop, and was a blessing upon getting back into the car. We then preceded to Walmart; again she was a blessing. When I got back home, I had a chance to sit back and think about things.

I had prayed that God would show me things because I felt that it is time for me to draw back from my male friend. I have discussed it with him on several occasions. Very sweet person, but feelings were getting involved and I had to pray to ask God to deter the feelings. Both of us always say that God does things in His time and according to His plan. I had been praying about drawing back, but every time I try to, it does not work. We're on the phone a great deal encouraging one another, sometimes praying for each other's guidance.

Early the next morning, God showed me a vision. At first, I heard a buzzing in my right ear. Then I saw someone release a white dove from their arm. I saw either bars from a jail cell or bars from a cage. But the matter troubled me to the point where I called my sister in Virginia to tell her about the dream. I needed to understand what this meant.

As I went about my day, my phone rang a couple times, it was my male friend, but I did not pick up. The third time I finally picked up and one of the things I had to do was clear matters up. He didn't explain why he had to hang up fast on yesterday. Although sometimes in our lives we can overthink a situation, but God always reveals what is going on. It may take time to get an answer, but He always does gives us an answer, whether it is yes or no. Thanks be to God.

I began crying out to God about this matter, but it was on me to go out walking and write more in my book, which I did. I made several phone calls, especially the one to my son. I wanted to make sure he was okay. His voice sounded better than it did when I saw him a few days ago. I asked him if he was hungry, he said "no" he does not have an appetite. He asked if he could call me back later. He didn't, but nevertheless, I still pray for him. Praying that God would turn things around on his behalf. I also spoke to the man that my son does work for. He still wants to take me out to dinner, but I am a little leery.

Sometimes it's hard to meet people. This is because some of the conversations are about sex. I don't like that! For that reason alone I pull back, especially if I'm just meeting a person; or any conversation about sex. I am not comfortable about that conversation at all. Why is it when a man (not all men), want to hold a decent conversation, they want to always bring up conversations involving sex. That makes me not to want to be bothered. Because if that's all you want to talk about, that means you're looking at me as a sex object and you're not interested in who I am. RED FLAG!! But God has been so good to me. I had to explain to him that I am not that type of person. He felt that there are times when a man has a need. I explained to him I know that but still I am not that person he will be having that need met with. And I let it go.

After thinking on all of this, I thought, maybe I don't need to be going anywhere with this man. I tell people, I don't do things for attention. Things such as dress, hair, nails, etc. I am my own individual and don't have to draw attention to myself. This is an area, where we as women have to stop doing. Not all women, but those that do feel as though they need a man to justify who they are.

We stand strong in our spot, just because we are women. When God created us, He allowed each of us to be beautiful in our own way. Some of the beauty is outwardly, some is facial, some hippy, some with larger or small breast, some with skinny or thick legs; but whatever the case may be, we are all different. Our personality makes us who we are. Nothing more or nothing less can change that. When we are confident in who we are, for whatever reason, it becomes a threat.

Why is it that others feel intimidated or seem to be threatened because by self-confidence? Our self-confidence came with struggles; of having to believe in oneself, just because. Because we're laughed at, we're mocked, we're falsely accused; and it draws attention. Not the type of attention as, "I want your man" but the attention as being strong in your spot. That we know who we are and needs no justification regarding the matter. *(This rose knows her position).*

I, was one of those who was mocked, laughed at, envied, you name it, I was called that. But one day God dealt with me about my image. He said that He made me who I am. He created me for His glory. I used to walk with my head held down. He told me, "Hold your head up and walk with your head up. I made you to be who I wanted you to be." From that day until today, I do just that. He lets me know what to wear. If my clothes become too tight, He always makes a way that I can get clothes that aren't tight, but fit nicely. Why can't we as women do that for each other? Why can't we give each other a compliment? Is that such a hard task? Why do some women want to put you down to feel good about themselves?

If you can't deal with another woman's confidence, then why don't you ask her, what did it take to get where she is? I'm sure, that the woman or women you ask will not have a problem telling you. Because a woman has confidence in herself, doesn't mean she's stuck up or haughty. It only means that she found her spot and her position as to who SHE is! Meaning, she found herself! But, overall, today was a good day.

Just logging events and my actions throughout the days. I have been inside of my apartment now off and on for a couple of weeks now due to this Coronavirus that seems to be an epidemic throughout this country. Nationwide it has hit almost every area in this world. Many are dying and becoming sick to the point where hospitals have to get beds setup in other rooms in different hospitals. Pastors are getting sick and some are dying with it, church members are getting sick and is listed in critical condition. Babies are sick with this virus, as well as animals are getting it.

One thing I know and can't speak for no one else is that God has given me a peace concerning it. I have been encouraging others that God don't want us to fear what is coming upon this earth. He said in *2 Chronicles 7:14 that, "If my people, which are called by my name, shall humble themselves, and pray, and seek my face, and turn from their wicked ways; then will I hear from heaven, and will forgive their sin, and will heal their land."*

This is where He is confirming His Covenant. He also mentioned in the verse before that, which is verse 13 that, *"If I shut up heaven that there be no rain, or if I command the locusts to devour the land, or if I send pestilence among my people....then He went into "If my people...."*

While this epidemic of this virus is taking place, we are also hearing about the locust devouring the land.

There are times when we don't want to take the Word of God serious, but what is it going to take for us to get serious about who God is? What is it going to take to realize that God is not playing? How long are we going to go about doing what we want to do and ignore the signs of the time? Have we REALLY forgotten who God is? Have Satan deceived the church and world to the point where we are now believing lies from others, verses believing what the Bible says? How long will you hearken between two opinions? Who are we anymore? These are questions we need to be asking ourselves.

Questions where now is the time to get these answers from God. There is an epidemic going around with this virus. Many and I mean many are dying. Many people, including Christians are afraid. They're going about to and fro seeking answers. Wondering when will this pass? When can we return to normal lives? It is now the beginning of April and this country has been dealing with this about a month. Not giving statistics, but it is overwhelming hearing the news all of the time. We have to believe God and take him at His word.

It was about 4 to 5 days ago when my brother asked me to help him move some of the items. I went over there on Wednesday to take down his curtains and whatever else I can do to help him out. It was also during that time that he was having a shortness of breath. His daughter and one of my great nephews were helping, so I went home. Not long afterwards, I received a call from him. He stated that his daughter called the doctor and He had an appointment the next day. But his doctor wanted him to go to the emergency room now. So, when he called, I went to his house to take him. He wanted me to drive his truck since I was used to driving it.

Upon arriving I went inside with him, but his great granddaughter and I could not go beyond the ER sliding doors. Eventually he called back stating that they want to keep him overnight. He really didn't want to stay. The next morning I called to check on him and he stated that he has pneumonia and a little fluid in his lungs. He also was a little upset because one doctor came in and told him that he had the virus. I don't know how the word got around, but I was receiving calls from family, telling me to quarantine myself and his great granddaughter. I was asked if I had any symptoms, and did he had any. Neither of us had any. Even my grandson whom I had not heard from for a while texted me stating, "Grandma, go home ASAP, etc." I felt that he was scolding me for being out in the public.

When I spoke to my daughter about it, she was laughing stating that he was really serious. She spoke to my oldest granddaughter also and she was upset too concerning my health. The both of us said, "Those March babies." But we know that we still had to be careful. My daughter stated that if I needed anything to let her know and she will go get it. I thank God for them showing love toward me.

During this time, from the day my brother went into the hospital, I had been staying at his new apartment with his great granddaughter. Putting things in its proper place so when he comes home, he would have very little, if anything to do. There were times where I had to scold her and put her on punishment because she just does things without asking and making a mess. But I try not to be so hard on her because my brother lets her do whatever she wants, so I backed off some. Not much though because she will try to rule me and the house at the age of 10 years old. I had informed my brother of how she was doing. And I informed him how she was helping out around the house. I did not give him any negative reports on her because he does not need to hear it right now. But she is still a child and times a child still needs to stay in a child's place and get corrected. Yet, I wanted him to remain as stress free as possible.

I spoke to my brother again tonight. He is still feeling a little down. I asked him if he is eating because when I spoke to him earlier, he said that he felt so weak. He also began saying that just in case things got worse, he had instructions he wanted me to follow. I didn't ask him if I could pray, I stated, "lets' pray" because the enemy was trying to give him a self-pity spirit of giving up. He stated how he wanted me to keep his granddaughter and not give her to her father because he really did not want her, and to tell her mother to fight for custody of her daughter. And in case he doesn't see us again, take care of things.

After talking to him again, he sounded about the same. I could tell both times that he was crying. My brother does not cry. But for the last several days, he had been crying. I prayed for him to take a hold of strength and that he is to look unto the hills from whence cometh his help, knowing that his help cometh from the Lord. I allowed his great granddaughter to speak to him at least twice a day. This helps him a great deal knowing that she is being well taken care of. *(This rose is under a lot of pressure).*

It was now Monday! Today I thank God for allowing me to wake up in my right mind. I started working on my emails to the kids in the program where I work.

I also had to send my supervisor and her assistant the first part of my weekly plan. Looking into trainings and other areas I had to deal with on my job was somewhat of a challenge, but I made it through.

My brother was still in the hospital and wanting to get out, saying that the food was so bad. I had to keep letting him know that although it's bad, he still had to get some type of nutrition in him in order for them to release him.

It was another day as well that my male friend called me, like he does every morning. Usually, I would be so upset to hear from someone every morning and sometimes 3 to 5 times a day, but for some reason it doesn't bother me when he calls. Talking about God's goodness and things such as this and ending in an "I love you" note.

It's going on now throughout the week getting up, getting my brother's great-granddaughter up, she's eating her breakfast, doing her homework, as well as me doing mine. It was later doing the week that my brother called from the hospital stating that his test came back and that he does not have the virus. Thank you Jesus! It was the end of the week he was released.

But for some reason, when I picked him up from the hospital on that Thursday, I came inside of his apartment, with him and his great granddaughter following me that a weight of tiredness came upon me like never before. The earlier part of the day I had cooked a pot of fresh lima beans with meat in it and some rice because I know how hungry he was and wanted some home cooked food. He only wanted a little bit because of his stomach getting adjusted to regular food again. So before I left, I fixed him some with a little rice in a small bowl. He took his time eating it, but he was still tired. I think he wanted me to stay, but I saw that his granddaughter was getting ready to act up and I was not going to deal with that, after dealing with her for about a week. But as I was getting ready to leave, I realized that he needed a shower curtain. I left to get him one and came back and put it up for him, then left. I was really exhausted when I got home.

It has been a somewhat crazy week for me, but I thank God that He took me through it. It was the end of the week now and my great granddaughter had a birthday. Something I wasn't able to do before was get her a present. So, I sent my granddaughter some money to help with her birthday party. As a grandmother, I felt good, because this little great granddaughter of mine is such a sweetheart.

Every time she sees me, she runs to me and hug me. I feel really good when I can be in their lives while they are so young. Realizing she never had the chance to meet her grandmother nor does she see her grandmother's mom; and if so, it's rarely.

It is now Saturday, when I got a call again from my brother. He wanted me to come sit with his great granddaughter while he went to the bank. I thought of him bringing her to my apartment, but I thought about the fish he said I could have, so I went there to do what he asked me and got me a couple bags of fish for myself. Upon him returning from the bank, one of my sisters pulled up. I stayed a little while and held a conversation with the both of them, then I left.

But one thing struck me, my brother made a statement of what his great granddaughter said. That was unusual for him because he always takes up for her, but he made the statement right in front of her and she felt a little embarrassed. I was happy because she can be a handful at times. It was also during this week that I received a call that one of my granddaughters were in the hospital. The doctor's weren't sure of what it was. At first, they diagnosed her as having air in her lungs; later diagnosing her as having a hole in her esophagus.

Thank God the nurse told me that it looked like it was healing itself and no surgery at this time was needed. She ended up being released a couple days later.

Now I'm going into the end of the week of the 17th, this is another day the Lord has made. I am so grateful God saw me through this week. It was another trying week for me. It seems like I've been bombarded with so much. But I won't complain, it could have always been worse. But God! (*This roses' struggle).*

Chapter Eighteen

"The Struggling Rose"

I haven't written in a while because of so much I've been going through. But God is taking me through. It was after the fact of my granddaughter being in the hospital and the following week my brother ended up back in the hospital. This time he had his great-granddaughter to call me to come over there to watch her. As I was asking her why, my brother than got on the phone and said, "I need help." I then, suddenly got up, got dressed, put me some clothes in a bag and went over there. And although a curfew was on for 8pm for everyone, I took a chance and went over there. It was after 10pm.

When I got there, he had a trash can in front of him where he had been throwing up blood. His daughter was already there and had already called the ambulance. Upon their arrival, they came in all suited down, from head to toe, I guess they were being cautious because of the virus that is going around. They had asked him to sit up, he again, began gagging and had to throw up again. He threw up more blood. I started praying. As they were taking his vitals, his body stiffened and he felt backwards, his eyes going into his head. I called on the blood of Jesus, and whatever he was going into, God brought him right out of it. Nobody but God.

The EMS questioned him to see If he remembered anything. He was able to answer all of the questions as asked. Thank God! I had gotten on the phone and began calling those that I knew would and could get a prayer through. One of the people was my male friend. As they were taking him out on the stretcher, they would not allow him to take anything with him, his eyeglasses, his robe, his phone or anything. I stayed at the house with his great-granddaughter while his daughter remained there for a while, then left.

The next day, I was too exhausted to do anything. My male friend had called me and recommended that I not have service because I was too exhausted and said that he was going to do the same thing. Which I actually was too exhausted. It wasn't until that afternoon that I took his great-granddaughter to her father. She wanted to go and at the time she was too much on me. After taking her to her father, I went back home and rested.

Getting up the next morning I began working on my assignment for Monday. Again, my male friend called me telling me that he loved me, as usual. But it was something I was beginning to pick up again. And I realized then that I had to let go. I was already having feelings for him, but I had to let go. It hurt but I felt that it was time.

It was later on during that week where I was in a conversation with him, that certain things he would say, and some things were not so hurtful as they were messing with my mind. I had explained to him before not to do that. And for some reason, some things he would say, God would let me know that it would be coming from another woman. But the last conversation I had with him bothered me. I called him back and asked him why was he playing with my mind? He just said, that I just wanted to know what you are thinking. But a woman knows another woman's injection and the Holy Ghost screens into a matter. It bothered me, so later on I text him and told him that I have to back off. I explained why. I had told him a while ago that I had to back off for the same reason, but he, at the time didn't want me too. But this time I had too, and I gave him several reasons why.

I let him know that although he would tell me every day that he was in love with me, but was it me he was in love with? Along with other things that God had given me discernment about; although before he denied it, but God kept giving me discernment about this other person and I told him. I asked him not to call me or I call him until he gets through this. And if I am the person God said is for him, then God will work it out, but until then he had to go through what he is dealing with concerning this other woman.

I explained to him in the beginning that I am not going to be THE OTHER woman in another relationship, and I meant it. Until he gets through this, I can't deal with him. If he decides that he wants to keep going on with this other person, he may as well say goodbye to me, and I moved on with my life.

And that let me know if all of the days he would tell me that he loved me and would always be there for me, was it for real or was I just being used as a decoy. I am not and will not let him or no one else hurt me again. But it was so strange that he was the one that helped me get through my hurt of abuse and turned right around and projected the same type of hurt to me again.

But I thank God that He showed me what I needed to do. And yes it hurt, but I had a peace about what I did. God let me know that he didn't know what he should do since he was exposed. God let me feel that he was dealing with what I had text him. He wanted to call but didn't know what to say. I prayed for him, but right now, that is all I can do, is pray. He had tried to call me a few times after I sent him that text. Discernment is a very important gift from the Holy Spirit and we must pay attention to it, and He will perfect it.

Although we hadn't talked, one day my finger accidentally hit his number. How? I don't know, but he instantly called back, that was 6 something in the morning. I text to let him know that it was where my finger accidentally hit his number and told him, "not yet." He still called back two other times and I would not pick up. And for some reason, when he called, I felt a pain of hurt go through me and I cried. I didn't understand why I felt that, but I did. Now, do I think about him, yes, do I miss him yes, and am I still in love with him, yes. But right now, I rather hold on to those feelings and not deal with him until God either correct him or remove him out of my life. And I know that I have to wait on God. And I do believe that God is not going to allow anyone into my heart again to hurt me and to play games with my mind like he was starting to do.

I had explained to him that what he was doing was a type of abuse, but he started going into another area of it. I explained to him again. And to me, if you love a person and trying to love someone else at the same time, someone is going to get hurt. I thank God He allowed me to notice that. So regardless as to whether or not I am hurting? I'd rather hurt this way by letting go, than to continue to hold on to someone I know who doesn't have my best interest at heart, although he says it all of the time. But to me, one's actions speaks louder than words.

And because a person is nice and quiet, doesn't mean that they are naïve. *(This rose was struggling with her feelings).*

Going into another week, all I can say is, this is another day that the Lord has Kept me. He has kept me from all evil, with my mind stayed on Jesus. This is another day that the Lord has kept me.

This week particularly was a hard week for me. I had a chance to talk to my male friend. I was tossed between walking away and or still standing to try and fight. I received a call again in the morning from my male friend and I was hurting and really tossed. My prayer had always been that God if this is what you want for me, than you have to work it out. But something changed. When I received a call this morning, he knew that I was tossed. But he mentioned something, to me, that really tossed my mind around and in a way mocked my feelings. I think this was the deal breaker.

I had recently been delivered from the pain of abuse, but then for him to turn around and do this? He was probably only kidding. But there are times a woman knows when something comes from another woman; whether through a behavior, words or actions. Especially if you know that this is not the person's normal behavior! But right then I knew that something had to change.

I tossed again during the night. But later that evening, I decided to write him a text, letting him know that I had to back off. I informed him in several ways why. I explained in the text about the love he always told me about on an everyday occasion. But asked him, was I the one he was in love with? I asked him not to call me and I not call him because, although I wasn't mad or upset with him, I just felt that there were things he had to get right. Not only with himself; not only with other people; but with God. I realized then that I could not and would not, any longer settle. Being told on an everyday basis that you're loved may mean the world to certain women. But I did not feel the sincerity of love towards me. There were days I felt it from him, but there were also days that I didn't.

I'm reminded about certain things. When God put something in your Spirit about something or somebody, He will not allow it to be shaken. There may be times you forget about it, but He always brings it back to your remembrance.

So as the week prolonged, which was the very next morning, he called. I felt like I had a broken heart and wanted to cry. I did not answer! He waited and called back a couple more times, I still did not answer. I made up in my mind that I had to stand my ground on this.

A week went by and it was on me to call. At first, I didn't know what to say, and neither did he. But I asked how he was doing; he asked me the same. I said that I had to call (didn't explain why) but that I had to. He said I'm glad you did. The phone call was very awkward, but it had to be done. I decided to let the past stay behind when he mentioned about a part of the text. I know what God showed me; but it wasn't a concern of his, but for me to let it go because the point was made. The both of us decided to remain friends and keep things on a spiritual level. Although, this was something I would always remind him of anyway.

Our connection was so much more spiritual. If anything comes out of it down the road, that it will be God's doing. If I needed prayer or anything, he said that he will always be there for me and I said the same. If we needed to talk, we'll talk but both of our feelings got caught out there. I knew that Satan really wanted me to get caught in this situation to bring embarrassment and humiliation to me. But God warned me in the very beginning of what to look out for concerning this person and what and how the enemy wanted to trick me.

I thank God I waited on Him.

I found out that it is so easy to love someone who is gentle, kind and loving to you. But once that person in anyway tries to harm you or thinking they're fooling you because you're so naïve, *(so they think)*; that you look at them in another way. But we have to remember that God always knows best. We ended up on the right key and the key to start afresh but on the Spiritual level.

Through my process of loving, I know that love isn't all the time love. Through my process of pain, that pain isn't always a thorn. But the remedy of what God's ways are in our lives. He never said that His way would be a bed of roses, but of sunshine and rain. So how could I see the rose pedals develop within me, if I had not of gone through the heartache of pain. Even still dealing with my son and other issues, this rose still have to develop in knowing how to lean on God!

This rose has struggled through many heartaches and through much pain. But is always growing into deeper depths and higher heights. This is because, when we seek God for answers through our hurt, He will always guide us through. When we're in a storm, He will help us to ride though the storm. He is the only one that can cause the storm to cease. By this we can tell if we're in the flesh or in the spirit. Looking unto Him to work things out and to carry us through our season.

Know that this rose has been kept and has been strengthened to continue in this walk of life.

A new chapter has just begun in my life!

May God tremendously bless you…..

A Rose from the Wikipedia says:

"Roses are best known as ornamental plants grown for their flowers in the garden and sometimes indoors. They have been also used for commercial perfumery and commercial cut flower crops. Some are used as landscape plants, for hedging and for other utilitarian purposes such as game cover and slope stabilization."

There are also rose thorns which are on the stem. These thorns are very sticky, meaning that they will cut you deeply. Roses also have green leaves surrounding the rose and down the stem. But there is something that God showed me this morning. He showed me the name of this book and the cover of this book. He showed me that I was that fighting rose.

I've been through the storms of life; I've been through the deserts and through the rains; I've been and took more pain from people than a normal individual. I accepted people for who they were, but, wasn't received as the same.

I've been lied on by pastors, ministers, bishops, evangelist, missionaries, friends, co-workers, family and of course, enemies. But through all of the pain, He showed me that I still came out smelling like a rose. A rose with honor and respect.

I've been laughed at, mocked, persecuted, discerned upon, pro-pho-lied to (*if that's a word*); falsely accused, mentally accused, picked on, scorned, you name it, and the list can go on and on. But through all of what I've dealt with, God STILL had me to stand.

There were many times I lost my faith; there were times when I got mad with God. There were times I wanted to give up; my hope failed me; my heart sank. Many, many, many and I mean many days I cried. And I know sometimes people look at me and tell me now how strong I was; but little did they know that those were the days when I felt like I was nothing. I didn't feel like dealing with people; sometimes I wouldn't and didn't answer my phone. Sometimes I didn't want anyone, not even my children knocking on my door. But no one, but God delivered me. So, when He gave me this title, He allowed things to become so obvious.

A rose can go through storms and still some of the petals remain standing.

There are times when the rose cannot handle the fire, and loses its petals, but the root of that rose continues to flourish. Flourish beyond recognition. To the point when a rose dies out, there is something about a rose that brings out the fragrance of glamour. This Fighting Rose found that out!

From one woman to another woman, become that rose that God created you to be.

"The Fighting Rose"

"A rose is so beautiful, Looking at it from eyes view, Beautiful, tender and lovely, rarely and deficiencies, if so, only a few.

The green lovely leaves unfolding, like holding it, on ones' hands, the spiking scorned stems, saying, touch me, if you can!

I'm a tender rose, I must say, everyone, can't feel my touch, I'm the gently yet bristle one, that everyone loves so much.

But once you doubt my tender touch, and reject my tender love, you will never know my beauty, or my soft leaves like a dove.

Oh why, can I not be so beautiful, when the wind and hail approach, why can't my soft leaves, blow so little, like a beautiful diamond broach?

I've fought through many battles, I've come through many storms, my petals still hanging bristly, through the munching of many worms.

Why can't you see my beauty, while holding me in your hand? I'm only a part of your beauty, and that's if, you're willing to stand.

So through my many battlegrounds, I've wept, stood strong and firm, by allowing my fragrance of glory, get affected by a germ.

As a reminder of your battles, don't give up by standing to doze, be sensitive of your sticking thistle, by going forward as "The Fighting Rose."

By Riva L. Green